THE NAVY CAPITAL OF THE WORLD

THE NAVY CAPITAL OF THE WORLD

HAMPTON ROADS

Amy Waters Yarsinske

Charleston · London

THE
History
PRESS

Published by The History Press
Charleston, SC 29403
www.historypress.net

First published 2010

Manufactured in the United States

ISBN 978.1.59629.973.3

Library of Congress Cataloging-in-Publication Data

Yarsinske, Amy Waters, 1963-
The navy capital of the world : Hampton Roads / Amy Waters Yarsinske.
p. cm.
ISBN 978-1-59629-973-3
1. Hampton Roads Naval Base (Va.)--History. 2. Hampton Roads (Va. : Region)--History,
Naval. I. Title. II. Title: Hampton Roads.
VA70.H36Y37 2010
359.709755'5--dc22
2010011270

Contents

Introduction

Contemporary historians have more often than not traditionally and remarkably omitted mention of the United States Navy in the same sentence with Hampton Roads. The exceptions to this are obvious, including narrative of the 1807 *Chesapeake-Leopard* affair that precipitated the War of 1812 and the March 9, 1862 battle of the ironclads that sounded the death knell of the sailing navy. Certainly, the lion's share of the navy's remarkable Hampton Roads achievements is slighted in narratives that focus on the milestone and not the place.

On November 1, 1767, Tory Scotsman Andrew Sprowle, merchant and ship owner, established his Gosport shipyard on the western shore of the Elizabeth River under the British flag. After the American Revolution began in 1775, Sprowle remained loyal to the British Crown and fled Portsmouth on the royal governor's flagship. Sprowle's properties were confiscated by the Virginia colony. When the British burned the yard four years later, it did not deter the new United States from restoring it to full operation. This former colonial shipyard thus became the navy's nucleus in Hampton Roads, where the largest naval base in the world has developed. The Norfolk Naval Shipyard is the United States Navy's oldest and actually predates the Department of the Navy by thirty-one years; it is also the largest shipyard on the East Coast. Known for most of its first century as Gosport Navy Yard, it was renamed Norfolk Navy Yard in 1862 after what was then the largest city in the region and has never borne the name of its home city of Portsmouth. But that is not all. Not for this storied shipyard, the first significant navy presence in Hampton Roads.

For more than 230 years, the Norfolk Naval Shipyard has helped the nation win nine major wars, put an end to piracy, send the Great White Fleet around the world, scientifically explore the Pacific and open Japan to American trade. The yard built the frigate USS *Chesapeake*, sister of the USS *Constitution* and one of the first six ships constructed for the United States Navy after the Revolutionary War. One hundred additional ships followed before the shipyard finished building its last ship, a wooden minesweeper, in 1953. Construction is now done elsewhere, like Newport News Shipbuilding and Dry Dock Company, founded by railroad magnate Collis Huntington in 1886 and located across Hampton Roads from Norfolk. Newport News Shipbuilding delivered its first ships to the navy in 1897.

At Gosport, the first dry dock in the western hemisphere opened on June 17, 1833, by hosting the seventy-four-gun ship of the line USS *Delaware*. Dry Dock No. 1, listed as a National Historic Landmark in 1971, remains in use today. It was at this yard, too, that the partly burned steam frigate USS *Merrimack* was converted by the Confederacy into the CSS *Virginia*, the world's first ironclad. The March 8–9, 1862 Battle of Hampton Roads garnered attention on both sides of the Atlantic when *Virginia* engaged the Union's wooden sailing ships USSs *Congress* and *Cumberland* and, later, the Federal ironclad USS *Monitor*. This two-day engagement changed naval technology, and strategic thinking, around the world.

The Norfolk Navy Yard built the sea service's first battleship, USS *Texas*; its first modern cruiser completely constructed by the United States government, USS *Raleigh*; and converted the collier USS *Jupiter* into the first ship designated an aircraft carrier, USS *Langley*. The latter was not the shipyard's first brush with naval aviation. Curtiss Exhibition Company pilot Eugene Burton Ely took off from the first flight deck built on a ship, furnished by the Norfolk Navy Yard. Ely's feat from the deck of the scout cruiser USS *Birmingham* (CL-2) took place November 14, 1910, nearly a full year before the official birth of United States naval aviation, and was front-page news around the world.

The Norfolk Naval Shipyard reached its peak employment of forty-three thousand workers during World War II, when it repaired 6,850 American and Allied warships and built nearly 30 more for the United States fleet. In addition to major warship construction, the yard would also build 20 tank-landing ships and 50 medium-landing craft. During the three-year Korean Conflict that followed, the shipyard completed work on more than 1,250 naval vessels and built 2 wooden minesweepers. These would be the last keel-up warships built at the Norfolk Naval Shipyard. By early 1965, it had attained nuclear technology capability when USS *Skate* (SSN-578) became the first modern submarine to undergo major overhaul in the yard.

The navy's development of its oldest and largest shipyard in Hampton Roads was only the beginning of more to come. Norfolk's Sewell's Point has become the site of the world's largest naval base. Portsmouth's Hospital Point is the site of the oldest naval hospital. The region is home to the East Coast's premier master jet base, Naval Air Station Oceana; the strategically important Joint Expeditionary Base Little Creek-Fort Story, the largest base of its kind in the world; and Fleet Combat Training Center Dam Neck, all located in Virginia Beach. And Collis Potter Huntington's private shipyard on the Virginia Peninsula wasn't to be outdone. Prior to its purchase by Northrop Grumman in 2001, Newport News Shipbuilding and Dry Dock Company was the largest privately owned shipyard in the country. Today, Newport News Shipbuilding remains one of only two shipyards in the nation capable of designing, building and servicing all types of nuclear-powered submarines and is the only yard that designs, builds and services the nation's nuclear-powered aircraft carriers. The Newport News shipyard has built over 70 percent of the United States Navy's current surface combatant fleet.

The naval heritage of Hampton Roads, rich and enduring, but always with an eye to the future, has served to advance this nation as a world power, at sea and in the air. Each generation since the Revolutionary War has promulgated naval strategy, technology and hardware, much of it from this important maritime region. While the history of United States Navy in Hampton Roads could fill several volumes, this book is intended to advance the story just one more step, one that carries forward the history of the United States Navy in what is, without question, the navy capital of the world.

The figurehead of the 1819 seventy-four-gun ship of the line USS *Columbus*, shown here circa 1910, was all that remained of the once-great warship. The high points of *Columbus*'s history bear mention. Clearing Norfolk, Virginia, on April 28, 1820, *Columbus* served as flagship for Commodore William Bainbridge in the Mediterranean until returning to Boston on July 23, 1821. More than two decades later, after embarking Commodore James Biddle, commander of the East Indies Squadron, it sailed on June 4, 1845, for Canton, China, where on December 31, Commodore Biddle exchanged ratified copies of the first American commercial treaty with China. At the end, *Columbus* lay in ordinary at Gosport Navy Yard until April 20, 1861, when it was sunk by withdrawing Union forces to prevent it falling into Confederate hands. *Courtesy of the Library of Congress Prints and Photographs Division.*

The first USS *Cumberland* was a heavily armed fifty-gun frigate commissioned on November 9, 1842. William Doughty, its designer, also added a fully armed spar deck to *Cumberland*. When the Civil War broke out, *Cumberland* was at the Gosport Navy Yard with orders to watch deteriorating conditions in Norfolk and Portsmouth. When Virginia seceded, *Cumberland* transported Union naval officers and sailors into Hampton Roads to safety. They had just scuttled and burned other ships at the navy yard on April 20, 1861, to preclude their capture. *Cumberland* made open sea and headed to Boston for repairs. *Cumberland's* ten-inch Dahlgren gun was removed and replaced with what many naval officers called a seventy-pounder rifle. Since there was no such gun in the navy inventory, it is likely that this was a sixty-pounder Parrott rifle. *Cumberland* was assigned to the North Atlantic Blockading Squadron at Hampton Roads, and while on duty March 8, 1862, it was rammed and sunk by the ironclad CSS *Virginia*. Currier & Ives published this hand-colored lithograph of *Cumberland* in 1848. *Courtesy of the Library of Congress Prints and Photographs Division.*

The history of a permanent United States Marine Corps presence in Hampton Roads can be traced back to the establishment of a Marine Guard at Gosport Navy Yard, later renamed the Norfolk Navy Yard. Twenty enlisted marines arrived there in April 1802 to provide security. With the exception of the period between 1804 and 1807, the marines maintained a continued presence at the navy yard until 1978. Part of the United States Marine Guard compound at the Norfolk Navy Yard included this house, shown on a real picture postcard mailed August 23, 1911. *Courtesy of the author.*

Currier & Ives published this period hand-colored lithograph of the close engagement between the USS *Monitor* and CSS *Virginia* that took place in Hampton Roads on March 9, 1862. *Courtesy of the Library of Congress Prints and Photographs Division.*

The *Brandywine*-class sailing frigate USS *Sabine*, built in 1855 and part of the Atlantic Blockading Squadron, actively searched the East Coast for Confederate commerce raiders during the war, including the hunt for Captain Raphael Semmes's CSS *Alabama*, later destroyed by the USS *Kearsarge* off Cherbourg, France, on June 19, 1864. *Sabine* was ordered to Norfolk, Virginia, in August 1864 as a training ship for navy apprentices and landsmen; it was photographed that December off Fort Monroe. *Courtesy of the Library of Congress Prints and Photographs Division.*

The USS *Newark* (C-1) was the first modern cruiser in the United States Navy. Laid down by William Camp and Sons, Philadelphia, Pennsylvania, on June 12, 1888, *Newark* was launched on March 19, 1890, and commissioned on February 2, 1891. *Newark* operated off the Atlantic Coast for ten months, taking part in maneuvers and exercises until it detached on December 8 for Norfolk Navy Yard to undergo a post-shakedown overhaul. It detached March 11, 1892, for the North Atlantic Squadron. *Newark* returned from a cruise to the Mediterranean and Adriatic Seas to participate in Hampton Roads's International Columbian Naval Rendezvous in 1893. *Newark* was decommissioned June 16, 1912, and stricken from the Naval Vessel Register ten days later. *Courtesy of the author.*

After its fitting out, the battleship USS *Nevada* (BB-36), lead ship of its class, joined the United States Atlantic Fleet on May 26, 1916. *Nevada* was a revolutionary addition to the fleet, the first second-generation battleship and first super-dreadnought in the United States Navy. The October 16, 1915 *New York Times* called it "the greatest afloat." *Nevada* eclipsed the tonnage and firepower of many of its sister battleships. But it was also the first to have triple gun turrets, oil-fired steam plants and, after a 1927 refit, a single funnel. *Nevada* is shown here at the Boston Navy Yard on March 23, 1916. *Courtesy of the Library of Congress Prints and Photographs Division.*

Just before America's entry into World War I, *Nevada* conducted numerous training cruises and exercises out of its Norfolk, Virginia base; it is shown here in Hampton Roads in 1917. "The Cheer Up" ship did not immediately head overseas when war broke out; *Nevada* would be the last American warship to join the fight, arriving in support of the British Grand Fleet two months before war's end. BB-36 survived Pearl Harbor, was repaired and participated in naval operations for the duration of World War II. With over three decades of service to the fleet, *Nevada* was decommissioned on August 29, 1946, and sunk off Pearl Harbor nearly two years later. *Courtesy of the Library of Congress Prints and Photographs Division.*

Airmen from Naval Air Station Hampton Roads competed against corpsmen from Naval Base Hospital Unit A at tug of war. The event was held on Field Day, March 1, 1918, at the site of old Chambers Field. *Official United States Navy Photograph.*

Rear Admiral Calvin Thornton Durgin receives a briefing from pilots on board the USS *Tulagi* (CVE-72) following their return from airstrikes against enemy targets in southern France during Operation Dragoon in August 1944. The *Casablanca*-class escort carrier was commissioned December 21, 1943, on the West Coast, where it ferried stores, aircraft and men back and forth to Hawaii. *Tulagi*'s Pacific stay was brief; it steamed through the Canal Zone for Norfolk, Virginia, to complete overhaul and carrier qualifications, arriving March 17, 1944. After carrying a load of Army Air Force planes to Casablanca in late May and early June, *Tulagi* headed back to Norfolk. Durgin came aboard at Narragansett Bay on June 30, 1944, as Task Group 27.7 commander just before the carrier turned east to join combat operations in support of the invasion of southern France. *Courtesy of the National Archives and Records Administration.*

Chapter 1

A New Navy and a New War

When the American Revolution ended in 1781, the Virginia and Continental navies disbanded, ships disposed of and personnel sent home. Gosport Navy Yard was used largely to service merchant vessels carrying the American flag to ports all over the world. But the threat of Barbary pirates seizing unprotected American ships, cargoes and crew in the Mediterranean trading corridor angered the public. Unprovoked acts of piracy would not be tolerated. But what to do about it? The United States had no naval force, and though raising one was brought to the attention of the United States Congress as early as 1791, it was not until March 27, 1794, that Congress passed *An Act to Provide a Naval Armament*. This act authorized the construction of six frigates, the first American naval vessels built since the Revolutionary War. The act did something else, too, something equally important: it founded the United States Navy. [The United States Navy officially recognizes October 13, 1775, as its birthday. This is the date that the Continental Congress voted to fit out two sailing vessels. This was the original legislation out of which the Continental navy grew and, as such, constitutes the birth certificate of the navy. The Continental navy evolved into the United States Navy created by the 1794 act.] Absent a Department of the Navy at that time, the new navy was administered by the secretary of war.

Since the federal government owned no shipyard just then, lease agreements were struck with yards to build navy ships under the supervision of their captains and government-employed naval contractors. Navy agents were put in charge of shipyards, and yard clerks were appointed to assist them. The navy's first six frigates were given the names USSs *United States,* *Constitution, President, Congress, Constellation* and *Chesapeake.* Each frigate was to have originally been designed with forty-four guns, but it was ultimately decided that the last three, *Congress, Constellation* and *Chesapeake,* would be finished with only thirty-six guns. In his December 27, 1794 report to the House of Representatives, President George Washington's secretary of war, Henry Knox, described the frigates, each warship's armament requirement, materials that would be used in their construction and how those materials might be obtained. He also explained that each frigate would be built in six different ports of the Union, one of which was Gosport, in Portsmouth, Virginia. Gosport would build the thirty-six-gun *Chesapeake.* Per Knox's plan, Gosport was leased from the Commonwealth of Virginia by the federal government. Captain Richard Dale, his reputation already established in the navy as Captain John Paul Jones's lieutenant aboard the *Bonhomme Richard* and for his role in the fight with HMS *Serapis,* a British frigate captured by the Americans during the war, was placed in charge of Gosport's construction department. William Pennock was designated the navy agent. Pennock, by virtue of his office, became custodian and administrator of the entire yard. While John Morgan had been provisionally appointed constructor, he was succeeded by Josiah Fox. This method of managing the yard was actually retained until about 1810, some nine years after Gosport became a federal navy yard.

No one foresaw *Chesapeake*'s construction dragging on for years. An agent was immediately dispatched to Georgia for the best pine, and by December 1795 two-thirds of its white oak frames had been cut and shaped and the lion's share of the frigate's material, including cedar and the pine from Georgia, was in store. But its keel, due to many delays, had not been laid when peace was declared in 1796 between the North African regencies, popularly called the Barbary States, and the United States. Further work on *Chesapeake* was thus suspended. But work commenced again when it was believed the threat of war with France was imminent. Congress created the Department of the Navy on April 30, 1798, and the laying of the keel for the *Chesapeake* took place that December 10. The new Navy Department ordered the purchase of some vessels and the construction of others. Commodore Richard Dale took command of one of them, the *Ganges,* the first of these vessels that sailed from Gosport in 1798. *Chesapeake* was launched from Gosport on December 2, 1799, commissioned in May 1800 and placed under the command of Captain Samuel Barron during the quasi-war with France. Given its early fits and starts, observers called the *Chesapeake* an unlucky ship from the moment it slipped into the Elizabeth River. By the time it launched in 1799, the *Chesapeake* had cost the navy $220,678.80. Though perceived as unlucky, it did capture the *Young Creole* during its first cruise to the West Indies in 1800 and remained off Bermuda until recalled in 1801.

The first secretary of the navy, Benjamin Stoddert, recognized that it would be more cost effective for the navy to purchase its own shipyards rather than rent space at privately owned facilities. Stoddert convinced Congress to fund the purchase of six established shipyards, including Gosport. The federal government purchased the 15.25-acre shipyard at Gosport from the Commonwealth of Virginia for $12,000; the deed was executed on June 15, 1801, by James Monroe, then governor of Virginia. This tract was situated in the northeast corner of the present shipyard; the first structures at Gosport were a spar shed, a timber shed and riverfront wharves. Prior to 1827, other buildings were enjoined to the original structures, including an office, a commandant's house, marine barracks, a brick storehouse that stood near the First Street gate, a powder magazine, a smithery and two large covered building-ways known as ship houses. In the center of the yard stood a large, two-story frame building used as a marine hospital and also as a rigging loft and gunners' storeroom. The original boundaries of the Gosport Navy Yard were the southern branch of the Elizabeth River to the east, Portsmouth's Lincoln Street to the north, Second Street to the west and a creek, now Slip Number One, to the south.

In 1803, Congress appropriated $10,000 for improvements to the Gosport Navy Yard, specifically for the construction of a warehouse and additional timber shed. These were built. With money left over, yard paymaster and noted Revolutionary War soldier Daniel Bedinger also ordered the construction of a brick perimeter fence to mark the yard's northern and western boundaries and a brick residence for the yard superintendent. The first superintendent's quarters was designed by William Pennock and completed in 1804. Pennock is also responsible for erecting the wall on the north and west sides of the yard. The wall was finished in 1805 and enclosed the yard all around with the exception of the east side, which was bounded by the river. By order of Pennock, the first superintendent to occupy the house completed in 1804 was Samuel Barron. The yard also quartered the United States Marine Guard, ordered to the yard in October 1801, which arrived in April 1802. The marine guard also added buildings to the yard for its use. The guard detached in August 1804 but was reestablished in November 1807. Squadrons under the command of Dale, Thomas Truxtun and Stephen Decatur were frequently repaired or fitted out at Gosport in the years leading up to the War of 1812, and other vessels, known well for their exploits at sea, were built or reconstructed at Gosport during this early period. Prior to 1810, the yard's administrative officers, who had sometimes been civilians, were called superintendents and navy agents, but on July 7, 1810, Commodore Samuel Barron was appointed the Gosport Navy Yard's first official commandant.

In early June 1807 the *Chesapeake* returned to Portsmouth to be fitted out. But while there, an unforeseen stroke of bad fortune unfolded. Seven men who had declared under oath that they were American citizens joined *Chesapeake*'s crew. No one questioned whether they weren't truthful. The *Chesapeake-Leopard* affair that followed on June 22 would take everyone back to the moment of his oath. Just before June 1807 two French frigates made their way into Norfolk to repair damages sustained during a storm. The French and British were at war, but since the United States did not take sides, both countries' vessels were permitted in and out of American ports for legitimate repairs but not to fight or hide from a superior force on the open sea. When the British navy discovered that French ships had gone to Gosport, the admiralty dispatched the fifty-gun HMS *Leopard* to lay in wait off the Virginia Capes to destroy them as they made their way out to sea. But it also happened that *Chesapeake*, under the command of Commodore James Barron, had just set out for the Mediterranean Sea to takes its place as flagship of the American squadron. On board were the seven sailors who'd sworn they were American citizens. As *Chesapeake* passed from the Elizabeth River into Hampton Roads and into the Chesapeake Bay, *Leopard*'s captain ordered a search of *Chesapeake* for deserted British seamen. Barron refused. *Leopard* fired on *Chesapeake*, boarded it and took away four of *Chesapeake*'s crew, three Americans and one British, claiming all were deserters. But the four unlucky "deserters" weren't the only casualties. *Chesapeake* had eighteen wounded and three killed. *Chesapeake* limped back into the protected waters of the Elizabeth River. But its losses made the American public angry. Newspaper editorials and public debate urged President Thomas Jefferson to take retaliatory action.

The *Chesapeake-Leopard* affair was not Barron's finest hour. At the time of the incident, Stephen Decatur was commander of the United States Navy's force in Norfolk. Four days later, on June 26, 1807, Decatur relieved Barron as commanding officer of the *Chesapeake*. Barron's court-martial followed in 1808. Secretary of the Navy Robert Smith had written Decatur on July 3, 1807, that by his June 26 letter, "I gave you command of the frigate *Chesapeake*. You are still to command her, and in addition you are to command all gun boats now at Norfolk, including those lately built there, and all the gun boats lately built at Hampton, and in Mathews County, Virginia." The postscript to this event, however, became as famous as the *Chesapeake-Leopard* incident: the duel between Barron and Decatur. One of Decatur's duties as commander of the force in Norfolk was to sit on the board of Barron's court-martial. Although Decatur and Barron had once been friends, Decatur agreed to a verdict that expelled Barron from the navy for five years. This event began a thirteen-year dispute that was sparked by comments Decatur made regarding Barron's crushing defeat at the hands of the *Leopard* and did not end until Barron killed Decatur in a Maryland duel on March 22, 1820.

Chesapeake didn't fare any better than its masters. Once repaired, this unlucky ship was hard-pressed to find a crew. But once it did, they, too, met with awful consequences. Captain James Lawrence, who commanded *Chesapeake* during the War of 1812 and on it met his death, was originally opposed to commanding the tainted frigate. When *Chesapeake* met HMS *Shannon*, captained by Philip Broke, off Boston on June 1, 1813, it proved no match for the more experienced British crew. Captain Lawrence was mortally wounded by small arms fire and taken below deck, but not before declaring the famous phrase that has carried through the United States Navy's history: "Don't give up the ship!" HMS *Shannon* came alongside, a skirmish on the *Chesapeake*'s deck ensued and it was captured and taken into Halifax, Nova Scotia, as a prize of war. But *Chesapeake* hadn't yet reached its worst humiliation. The frigate's ignoble end finally came at the hand of a miller in Wickham, in Hampshire, England, who'd bought the prize of war from the British admiralty and broke it down for timber to build a flour mill.

The *Chesapeake-Leopard* affair, often called the Douglas War for Commodore John E. Douglas, commander of the British Fleet in Hampton Roads in the summer of 1807, turned out to be the opening salvo of another war with Great Britain. Tolerance for British bad behavior waned quickly, and back at home, the British blockade of American ports had severely curtailed merchant trade to Europe and the Caribbean. President James Madison sent a war message to Congress on June 18, 1812. During this time, Gosport Navy Yard had little protective force except a flotilla of poorly manned small gunboats. The frigate USS *Constellation*, dispatched as little more than a show of force, was prevented from putting to sea through the Virginia Capes by a large British blockading squadron. With great difficulty, the *Constellation* was kedged to a position in the Elizabeth River opposite Fort Norfolk, where it furnished detachments of seamen and marines to reinforce the harbor's weak defenses. Gosport's capture was never an option and, with the aid of local militia and regular forces, thus prevented. The Americans' success repelling British forces at the Battle of Craney Island in June 1813 ensured that the British flag would never fly again over the Gosport Navy Yard.

After the War of 1812, Gosport Navy Yard was expanded and its facilities improved. Certainly, the highlight of this was the keel laying of the ship of the line USS *Delaware*, the first of its kind ever built there, in 1817. *Delaware* was launched on October 21, 1820. But there was more to come. The HMS *Alert*, the first British man-of-war captured in the War of 1812, was assigned to the yard as its first receiving ship in June 1818, and three years later, in August 1821, a school for midshipmen was established there aboard the forty-four-gun USS *Guerriere* with Chaplain David P. Adams in charge. The school was the vision of yard commandant Commodore Lewis Warrington.

Importantly, in 1825 Secretary of the Navy Samuel Southard authorized a study of the navy's shore facilities to identify potential sites for the department's first two dry docks. The cost of land acquisition required for dry dock construction at first moved Southard to abandon the project. Plans for navy dry dock construction were revived by Gosport's commandant, Commodore James Barron, who argued that construction delays at the yard could be attributed to the lack of a dry dock. Water and Toredo worms—the termites of the sea that inhabited it—led to rapid decomposition of wooden wharves, which in turn left submerged remains that impaired navigation. The following year, after a survey of Portsmouth, New Hampshire; Boston; New York; and Gosport, Congress selected Boston and Gosport shipyards as the locations of the nation's first dry docks. Necessary improvements to both yards were authorized on March 3, 1827, when Congress passed *An Act for the Gradual Improvement of the Navy of the United States*, an initiative that gave the navy a half-million dollars per year for a period of six years to upgrade shore facilities.

Gosport was expanded. The navy's agent, a Mr. King, reported on March 25, 1827, that "the lands from [Portsmouth's] Jefferson Street, along the line of Third Street to the [Norfolk] county road, and thence down to the water, could be purchased for $7,825." King was authorized to purchase the parcel and procure as much land to the south of the yard as he thought necessary. The Board of Naval Commissioners developed a plan for the expansion of Gosport during the winter of 1827, predicated on a facility survey conducted by Loammi Baldwin Jr., considered the father of American civil engineering and son of noted engineer Colonel Loammi Baldwin. It is the younger Baldwin who accepted the appointment of the United States government in 1827 to construct the two great works of his career—the naval dry docks at Charlestown, Massachusetts, and Gosport. Forty-three town lots were subsequently bought by the Gosport navy agent between 1826 and 1829. The total purchase price was $23,622.

Begun in 1827 and finally completed in 1834, Gosport's dry dock, Loammi Baldwin Jr.'s masterpiece, was built of huge blocks of Massachusetts granite and cost $974,365.65, a large sum at that time. Before the dry dock was formally completed, it was christened on June 17, 1833, by the reception of the ship USS *Delaware*, the first vessel to be dry-docked in the United States. The ceremony, in keeping with the importance of the occasion, was attended by many national figures, including President Andrew Jackson and members of his cabinet, and attracted widespread attention. During this period, four hundred men worked at the yard, laboring over *Delaware* and *New York*. But *New York* was never finished and still rested in the stocks until it was set on fire in April 1861. After *Delaware* was finished, it bore a figurehead that represented Tecumseh, Indian chief of the Delaware tribe, which had been carved by a Portsmouth woodworker named William Luke.

By 1837, Gosport employed 1,200 men. Berthed at its docks were ships fitted out for one of many exploring expeditions that got their start there, among them the USSs *Delaware*, *Relief*, *Consort* and *Pioneer* and the schooner *Pilot*. Also at the pier was the thirty-eight-gun frigate USS *Macedonian*, a magnificent ship and Decatur's prize of war that Gosport rebuilt from the keel in 1836. It was from Gosport, too, that Commodore Matthew Calbraith Perry went out on the side-wheel steamer *Susquehanna* on June 8, 1851, to join his fleet bound for the East. *Susquehanna* became the flagship of Perry's Black Fleet on July 8, 1853, entering Tokyo Bay with his squadron on the momentous occasion of the opening of Japan to western trade.

After the yellow fever epidemic of 1855 that struck Norfolk and Portsmouth hard, the Gosport Navy Yard did recover. The frigates USSs *Roanoke* and *Colorado* were launched. The *Dakota* was built soon after, followed by the sloop USS *Richmond* in 1860. *Richmond* would serve in three wars, first the Civil War, then as a receiving ship in the Spanish-American War and finally as quarters for the commandant of the naval training station at Saint Helena during World War I. Among the many events that marked *Richmond*'s lengthy history, there is one that none other could claim: it was the last ship completed at the Gosport Navy Yard before the outbreak of the Civil War.

The frigate *Chesapeake* was the progeny of a January 2, 1794 House of Representatives resolution "that a Naval force adequate to the protection of commerce of the United States against Algerine [*sic*] corsairs ought to be provided." Six frigates were built: *United States, Constellation, Constitution, President, Congress* and *Chesapeake*. *Chesapeake* was built at Gosport Navy Yard, which became a federal shipyard in 1801. The keel was laid December 10, 1798, and it was launched December 2, 1799, and commissioned on May 22, 1800, under the command of Captain Samuel Barron. The largest and most important difference between *Chesapeake* and the other frigates was its size. *Chesapeake*'s length had been shortened to 152 feet, 6 inches; its beam to 40 feet, 11 inches; and it had been lightened to 1,244 tons. *Chesapeake*'s armament was reduced from forty-four guns to thirty-six and eventually increased to thirty-eight. These changes created a ship 13 percent shorter than the *Constellation* and *Constitution* but with a wider beam that made it heavier and slower. *Chesapeake* was captured by the British frigate HMS *Shannon* off Boston on June 1, 1813, a scene immortalized by Robert Dodd's 1813 print, shown here. *Courtesy of the Library of Congress Prints and Photographs Division.*

The USS *Hornet* was originally a 441-ton brig-sloop commissioned in October 1805 at Baltimore, Maryland. *Hornet* operated extensively on the East Coast and in the Mediterranean. The 1811 naval architecture drawing shown here is the stern of the *Hornet*, part of a series used to convert the brig-sloop to a sloop of war at the Washington Navy Yard that year. *Hornet* went down in a gale on September 29, 1829, off Tampico, Mexico, with its entire complement. *Courtesy of the Library of Congress Prints and Photographs Division.*

Under the command of another Barron, Commodore James Barron, *Chesapeake* was attacked by British frigate HMS *Leopard* off Cape Henry on June 22, 1807, an incident that led to the War of 1812. George Cruikshank published this hand-colored etching, a cartoon, that featured the *Leopard*'s boarding party routing the crew of *Chesapeake* on September 1, 1813. *Chesapeake*'s capture was a low point for America's fledgling navy. Barron was born in Hampton, Virginia, the son of a merchant captain named James Barron, who became commodore of the small Virginia States Navy during the American Revolution. *Courtesy of the Library of Congress Prints and Photographs Division.*

The first USS *Macedonian* was a United States Navy thirty-eight-gun sailing frigate, originally the HMS *Macedonian* of the Royal Navy, captured by Commodore Stephen Decatur, captain of the USS *United States*, on October 25, 1812, during the War of 1812. The British put to sea with the 156-foot *Macedonian* in September 1810. Claimed as a prize of war, *Macedonian* was pressed into service against the British blockading fleet off New York and, later, Mediterranean anti-piracy operations. *Macedonian* departed Norfolk on June 11, 1826, for service on the Pacific station, returning to Hampton Roads on October 30, 1828; it was decommissioned shortly thereafter and broken up at the Norfolk Navy Yard. *Courtesy of the Library of Congress Prints and Photographs Division.*

Commodore Stephen Decatur was a beloved figure to the people of Norfolk, Virginia. He married Susan Wheeler, daughter of Norfolk's mayor, on March 8, 1806. It was at Norfolk's Exchange Hotel that Decatur made his famous pronouncement: "Our country! In her intercourse with foreign nations, may she always be in the right, and always successful, right or wrong." Decatur's glorious and storied naval career ended at Washington, D.C., on March 22, 1820, when he was shot to death in a duel with rival Commodore James Barron. *Courtesy of the Library of Congress Prints and Photographs Division.*

The figurehead of the USS *Macedonian* was photographed by George Grantham Bain between 1910 and 1915. *Courtesy of the Library of Congress Prints and Photographs Division.*

Portsmouth Naval Hospital, without its dome, was photographed in 1902 by William Henry Jackson. Begun in 1827 and completed in 1830, it remains the oldest naval hospital in the United States. Situated on the Elizabeth River and devoted to the treatment of sick and wounded sailors and marines, the hospital was built on the site of Fort Nelson of War of 1812 fame. Inscriptions on the tombstones in the hospital's cemetery contain the names of men attached to the earliest ships of the United States Navy and battles in which those ships engaged. *Courtesy of the Library of Congress Prints and Photographs Division.*

The 1854 sloop of war USS *Constellation* was the second United States Navy ship to bear this name. The Naval Vessel Register indicates that the original frigate *Constellation* was disassembled on June 25, 1853, at Gosport Navy Yard, and the sloop of war was built in the same yard, possibly with recycled materials from its namesake frigate. Launched on August 26, 1854, and commissioned on July 28, 1855, *Constellation* was the last sail-only warship designed and built by the United States Navy. It is shown here in 1914. *Courtesy of the Library of Congress Prints and Photographs Division.*

This view of the main battery on the gun deck of the sloop of war USS *Constellation* was taken in 1914. *Constellation* carried sixteen eight-inch chambered shell guns; four thirty-two-pounder long guns; one twenty-pounder Parrott rifle (stern); one thirty-pounder Parrott rifle (bow); three twelve-pounder bronze boat howitzers; and spar deck pivot guns. *Courtesy of the Library of Congress Prints and Photographs Division.*

The first USS *Pennsylvania*, the largest sailing warship ever built for the United States Navy, was a three-decked 120-gun ship of the line and the equivalent of a first-rate of the British Royal Navy. Remarkably, its only cruise was a single trip from Delaware Bay to Chesapeake Bay. *Pennsylvania* was one of "nine ships to rate not less than 74 guns each" authorized by the United States Congress on April 29, 1816. *Pennsylvania*'s keel was laid at the Philadelphia Navy Yard in September 1821, but a tight budget slowed its construction, preventing it being launched until July 18, 1837. After its cruise into the Chesapeake Bay, *Pennsylvania* remained in ordinary until 1842, when it became a receiving ship for the Norfolk Navy Yard. This magnificent warship was burned to the waterline on April 20, 1861, to prevent capture by the Confederacy. The March 16, 1861 *Harper's Weekly* carried this wood engraving of the *Pennsylvania* anchored off the Gosport Navy Yard. *Courtesy of the Library of Congress Prints and Photographs Division.*

The USS *Portsmouth*, a sloop of war commissioned November 10, 1844, and struck from the navy registry on April 17, 1915, was designed by Josiah Barker and constructed on the lines of a French-built privateer at Portsmouth Navy Yard, Portsmouth, New Hampshire. *Portsmouth* set sail from Norfolk, Virginia, on January 25, 1845, on a cruise around Cape Horn to join the Pacific Squadron. When it returned to the East Coast in 1878, it was to serve as a training ship. *Portsmouth* was photographed by George Grantham Bain on Dewey Day, September 29, 1899. *Courtesy of the Library of Congress Prints and Photographs Division.*

Matthew Fontaine Maury was known as the "Pathfinder of the Seas and Father of Modern Oceanography and Naval Meteorology," and later "Scientist of the Seas," after publication of his landmark works on these subjects, most especially *Physical Geography of the Sea* in 1855, the first extensive and comprehensive book on oceanography to be published. Maury made many important new contributions to charting winds and ocean currents, including ocean lanes for passing ships at sea. When the Civil War broke out, he resigned his commission as a United States Navy commander and joined the Confederacy. He is shown here as a commander, Confederate States Navy. Norfolk's Matthew Fontaine Maury High School is named in his honor. *Courtesy of the Library of Congress Prints and Photographs Division.*

The sloop of war USS *Hartford*, shown here in 1905, was launched November 22, 1858, at the Boston Navy Yard. Later, when the Civil War broke out, *Hartford* was recalled from the Far East to return to the East Coast to be refitted for war. On January 28, 1862, *Hartford* emerged from the Delaware Capes as flagship of Rear Admiral David Glasgow Farragut, the commander of the newly created West Gulf Blockading Squadron. Farragut led the Federal fleet to victory at the August 5, 1864 Battle of Mobile Bay, arguably one of the most significant naval engagements of the Civil War. *Hartford*'s tie to Norfolk, Virginia, occurred at the end of its service life. Placed out of commission on August 20, 1926, *Hartford* was kept at Charleston until moved to Washington, D.C., on October 18, 1938. From there, on October 19, 1945, it was towed to Norfolk Navy Yard and classified as a relic. Sadly, *Hartford* was allowed to deteriorate and sank at its berth on November 20, 1956. Beyond salvage, it was dismantled. *Courtesy of the Library of Congress Prints and Photographs Division.*

Rear Admiral David Glasgow Farragut, photographed during the Civil War, is known as the first rear admiral, vice admiral and full admiral of the United States Navy. He is popularly quoted as having given the order at the Battle of Mobile Bay, "Damn the torpedoes, full speed ahead!" Born July 5, 1801, Farragut's naval career began at age nine, when he was taken under the tutelage of Captain, later Commodore, David Porter aboard the frigate USS *Essex*. Porter adopted Farragut in 1808, and he saw his first action during the War of 1812. *Essex* captured so many British vessels that at age twelve Farragut received his first command, a former British whaling ship. This storied officer died August 14, 1870. *Courtesy of the Library of Congress Prints and Photographs Division.*

Chapter 2
Brother Against Brother

Across the nation, newspapers of 1859 and 1860 sounded repeated notes of warning that war was coming—not a war against a foreign enemy but one between America's North and South. Headlines became reality on April 18, 1861, when Virginia seceded from the Union. Two days later, word of the secession reached the Gosport Navy Yard. Turmoil ensued. Portsmouth wasn't a southern stronghold. The navy yard was a bastion of the United States Navy, and many of the city's most well-respected citizens and the lion's share of its skilled workers had come from northern states. Exulting cheers mingled with the groans of those who realized almost immediately that lifelong friends would become enemies and families might be divided brother against brother.

Confusion reigned at the Gosport Navy Yard, which the Commonwealth of Virginia claimed as its rightful possession. Soon after workers left the yard at noon on April 20, the yard's commandant, Commodore Charles S. McCauley, had the gates secured to the public. McCauley was by then too old and anxious to cope with the turn of events that had now put him in the untenable position of protecting the navy's finest shipbuilding facility from the local population. Back in Washington, Secretary of War Gideon Welles had every reason to fear that Gosport would fall into the hands of Virginia troops. He quickly dispatched one hundred marines from Washington, D.C., on April 19, 1861, with orders to destroy the facilities at Gosport and retrieve the ships stationed there. The marines arrived as McCauley was boarding the USS *Cumberland* in Hampton Roads. He'd already evacuated the yard. McCauley would later be severely criticized for his hasty retreat.

But McCauley's critics likely, just then, knew little of what precipitated his action. In truth, his rapid evacuation was owed to General William "Billy" Mahone, president of the Atlantic, Mississippi and Ohio Railroad, precursor of the Norfolk and Western, and a staunch Southerner who'd joined the Confederacy at the moment of secession. He'd staged the ruse that hastened McCauley's retreat from Gosport. A lookout in the crow's nest of the USS *Delaware* saw trainload after trainload of Confederate soldiers brought to the outskirts of Norfolk on the Portsmouth side. Thousands of them, as far as the lookout could tell, had disembarked. But was it really thousands? No. Mahone brought his soldiers into town on rail cars standing up and then sent them out lying down in the cars, repeating the procedure enough times to fool the *Delaware*'s lookout. All night, Mahone's troops moved back and forth from Petersburg, sometimes with band playing and colors flying, all for show.

Before McCauley abandoned Gosport, Norfolk and Portsmouth's citizens worried that Federal troops intended to bombard both cities from the harbor. But this wasn't the navy's intention. McCauley had already reached an agreement with Virginia Militia commander Major General William Booth Taliaferro, who had taken command of Norfolk and Portsmouth on April 18, 1861, that there should be no bombardment, provided the harbor was not blocked. This agreement was strictly kept. A mass meeting of citizens was subsequently held, and a small committee was appointed to confer with McCauley to keep turmoil from turning to terror. As they approached the gate, the committee was met by a wave of officers who'd just resigned their United States Navy commissions. They told the committee that McCauley would not see them, and this was true. The date was April 20, 1861. Morning became evening. At dusk, the USS *Pawnee* sailed into port, its band playing the national anthem, colors flying and cannon loaded and ready to fire. That evening, the *Pawnee* opened up on Gosport on the order of its commanding officer, Captain Hiram Paulding. Paulding had been issued the order to burn the yard and contents, and when he'd fired as much of it as he could from the *Pawnee*, he and his men were to join the wrecking force in the yard, where marines had already set charges and begun scuttling the navy's ships in the Elizabeth River. Many United States Navy vessels were burned that day, with two remarkable exceptions: Stephen Decatur's USS *United States*, which had captured the *Macedonian* in one of the most thrilling exploits in navy history, and the USS *Cumberland*, which had been towed safely into the harbor. But the USSs *Dolphin*, *Plymouth*, *Raritan*, *Germantown*, *Merrimack* and *Pennsylvania* were burned to the waterline. Why McCauley's sailors did not set fire to the *United States* was never known. Several of the charges set by sailors and marines did not detonate; some contemporary reports credit Confederate sympathizers among McCauley's junior officers as responsible for the incomplete demolition of the yard and sparing of the *United States*. Captured by the Confederates, the *United States* was pressed into service as the receiving ship CSS *United States*. *United States*' service to the South was brief. Retreating Confederate forces sunk it when they abandoned Norfolk in May 1862. Though later salvaged by the United States Navy, it was determined the *United States* was not worth saving.

The April 1861 firing of the Gosport Navy Yard was a terrifying event. Hundreds of oxen and horses had been burned alive, and what could not be burned was destroyed by other means. Stores were thrown overboard and heavy cannon spiked. When the liquor supplies were poured out, so many of the sailors and workmen became drunk that they were unable to do their work properly, and some of the larger guns were not spiked well enough to keep Confederate troops from returning them to service. Just before dawn, the navy yard was a seething mass of flames, as ships of the line fell prey to the conflagration. Adding to the horror of the scene was the booming of the *Pennsylvania*'s loaded guns that fired off, bathed in the intense heat of the flames that consumed the largest sailing ship ever built for the United States Navy. As daylight broke, the navy yard was reduced to blackened ruins. But from those ruins the Confederate flag was raised, and Captain French Forrest took command. Forrest's executive officer was Captain Sidney Smith Lee, brother of General Robert Edward Lee. But it was only as daylight came that Forrest and Lee knew how lucky they'd been to capture the yard's dry dock intact. A trail of powder had been laid leading to a culvert at the dry dock's northwest corner where explosives had been rigged to destroy it. When water was later let into the dry dock, roughly thirty barrels of powder floated out. The order to destroy the dry dock hadn't been carried out.

Confederate forces who occupied the Gosport Navy Yard on April 21, 1861, found it badly damaged but otherwise serviceable. No time was wasted repairing the yard and raising the *Plymouth*, *Dolphin*, *Germantown* and *Merrimack* from their watery graves. Work on the first three started at once, but the *Merrimack* was at first rejected as worthless. On July 12, 1861, that assessment changed. *Merrimack* thus became the subject of one of the most revolutionary experiments in the history of naval warfare: it would undergo conversion from frigate to ironclad. The work had to be done quickly and in secrecy. Iron plates used to cover its hull were fashioned from train rails. *Merrimack* wasn't the only ship to undergo this transformation. There was the *Richmond*, another ironclad ship, as well as the gunboats *Hampton*, *Nansemond*,

Elizabeth and *Escambia*. Many of the Dahlgren and other guns left behind at Gosport were rifled and reused aboard the South's ironclad fleet. In early March 1862, the *Merrimack* emerged from the Gosport Navy Yard as the CSS *Virginia*. Built at Gosport under the direction of Portsmouth native son John Luke Porter, chief naval constructor of the Confederate States Navy, this amazing vessel sailed quietly down the Elizabeth River on March 8 to fight a battle that would revolutionize warfare.

While there have been many accounts of the CSS *Virginia*'s place in naval history, the one most poignantly and vividly told was by Henry Ashton Ramsay, the *Virginia*'s chief engineer, in the February 10, 1912 issue of *Harper's Weekly*. "The *Merrimack* was built in 1856 as a full-rigged frigate of thirty-one tons burden, with auxiliary steam power to be used in case of headwinds," Ramsay recounted. "She was a hybrid from her birth, marking the transition from sail to steam, as well as from wooden ships to ironclads. I became her second assistant engineer in 1859, cruising around the Horn and back to Norfolk. Her chief engineer was Allan Stimers." Ramsay remembered, too, that little did the *Merrimack*'s crew dream that Stimers would become the right-hand man of Swedish engineer John Ericsson, constructor of the USS *Monitor*, "while I was to hold a similar post in the conversion of our own ship into an ironclad, or that in less than a year we would be seeking to destroy each other, he as the chief engineer of the *Monitor*, and I in the corresponding position on the *Merrimack*." Captain Ramsay went on to observe that after the *Merrimack* was set on fire in April 1861, workmen scuttled it, which put out the fire. When raised by the Confederates, he noted that naval officers were "skeptical as to results." The iron plates that covered *Merrimack* were rolled at the Tredegar Iron Works in Richmond, Virginia, and arrived so slowly, Ramsay recalled, "that we were nearly a year finishing her. We could have rolled them at the yard here and built four *Merrimacks* in that time had the South understood the importance of a navy at the outbreak of the war."

Merrimack was full of workmen hurrying it to completion when Commodore Franklin Buchanan arrived from Richmond on a brisk March morning and ordered everything and everyone out of the ship except its crew. His next order was to his executive officer, Lieutenant Catesby ap Roger Jones, to prepare to sail at once. As the former navy frigate slipped into the Elizabeth River, it became CSS *Virginia*. Making its way down the Elizabeth, Ramsay could make out Newport News in the distance. There his eye trailed to gleaming Federal batteries and row after row of white tents that dotted the shore. Then he saw the Union's blockading fleet at the mouth of the James River, the masts of the USSs *Congress* and *Cumberland* piercing the sky high overhead, every line and spar clearly defined, their decks and ports bristling with guns. The *Cumberland*'s rigging was gay with red, white and blue sailors' garments hung out to dry. But after *Virginia* was sighted, *Congress* shook out its topsails and down came *Cumberland*'s clothesline.

"Our crew was summoned to the gun deck, and Buchanan addressed us," Ramsay recalled later, telling his men, "Sailors, in a few minutes you will have the long looked for opportunity of showing your devotion to our cause. Remember that you are about to strike for your country and your homes. The Confederacy expects every man to do his duty. Beat it to quarters." As the CSS *Virginia*, née *Merrimack*, approached the Federal fleet, it was met by a barrage of fire that Ramsay observed would have sunk a conventional wooden vessel, "except the *Merrimack*. They struck our sloping sides, were deflected upward to burst harmlessly in the air, or rolled down and fell hissing into the water, dashing the spray up into our very ports. As we drew nearer the *Cumberland*, above the roar of the battle, rang the voice of Buchanan: 'Do you surrender?' 'Never, I'll sink alongside,'" came the reply from *Cumberland*'s executive officer, Lieutenant George Upham Morris. "The crux of what followed was down in the engine room," Ramsay recorded later. "Two gongs the signal to stop, were quickly followed by three, and the signal to reverse. There was an ominous pause, then a crash, shaking us all off our feet. The engine labored. The vessel was shaken in every fiber. Our bow was visibly depressed. We seemed to be bearing down with a weight on our prow," he continued. "We had rushed on the doomed ship, relentless as fate, crashing through her heavy barricade of spars and torpedo fenders, striking her below her starboard forechains and crushing into her." For a moment, he would observe, the whole weight of the *Cumberland* hung on the *Virginia*'s prow, threatening to carry it down with the stricken Federal sloop, the return wave of the collision hurling up the *Virginia*'s port bow. The *Cumberland*, with heavy casualties on board, began to sink slowly bow first and continued to fight desperately for some forty minutes after its fate was sealed. "We had left our cast iron beak in the side of the *Cumberland*," Ramsay recounted. "Like the wasp we could sting but once, leaving the sting in the wound."

"Our smokestack was riddled and our flag shot down several times," Ramsay continued. The flag was finally secured to a rent in the stock. On the gun deck, the *Virginia*'s crew fought ferociously, giving little thought to the wounded and dying, he would recall later, as they tugged away at the guns, training and sighting their pieces, while the orders rang out, "Sponge, load, fire." At times, there would be the cry, "The muzzle of my gun has been blown away," to the reply by Catesby Jones, "No matter, keep on loading and firing. Do the best you can with her." The gunners aboard *Virginia* were covered with powder grime, so much so that Ramsay described them as "looking like negroes. Human hearts were beating and bleeding there, human lives were being sacrificed. Pain, death, wounds, glory—that was the sum of it." On the doomed ship *Cumberland*, the battle raged with equal fury. The sanded deck was red and slippery with blood. Delirium seized the crew, who cheered and fought as their ship sunk beneath Hampton Roads. As it listed, a pivot gun broke loose, leaving a mass of mangled flesh in its wake. Then *Virginia* went after *Congress*. Though the Federal frigate tried to escape, it ran aground, and after desperate firing came the order to surrender.

"The whole scene," recalled Ramsay, "was changed. A pall of black hung about the ships and obscured the clean outline of the three frigates, *Saint Lawrence*, *Roanoke*, and *Minnesota*, also enveloped in the clouds of battle that now and then reflected the crimson lightning of the god of war." The masts of the *Cumberland* protruded above the water. The *Congress* presented a terrible scene of carnage. The gunboats CSS *Beaufort* and CSS *Raleigh* were summoned to take off the wounded and fire the ship. But they were driven away by sharpshooters on shore who suddenly turned their fire on the *Virginia*, ignoring the white flag of the *Congress*. Buchanan fell, severely wounded in the groin. While being carried below deck, he instructed Jones, "Plug hot shot into her [the *Congress*] and don't leave her until she is on fire. They must look after their own wounded since they won't let us." Buchanan's brother was paymaster on the *Congress*.

After the *Congress* was fired, the *Virginia* next went after the three frigates, but all made off except for the *Minnesota*, which pulled out of *Virginia*'s reach. *Virginia* laid up at Sewell's Point for the night. The following morning, March 9, *Virginia* planned to destroy the *Minnesota*. But that's not what happened. "We left our anchorage shortly before eight o'clock in the morning," Ramsay remembered later, "and steamed across and upstream toward the *Minnesota*, thinking to make short work of her. We approached slowly, feeling our way along the edge of the channel, when suddenly a black object that looked like the historic description, 'a barrel head with a cheese box on it,' moved slowly out from under the *Minnesota* and boldly confronted us." The great fight was on, a fight the likes of which the world had never seen before, when "the battle of yesterday" passed away, and with it the experience of "a thousand years of 'battle and of breeze'" was brought to an end. The books of all navies were burned with the *Congress*, Ramsay would rightly observe, by a conflagration as ruthless as the torch of Omar. "We hovered about each other in spirals, gradually contacting the circuits until we were in point-blank range, but our shells glanced from the *Monitor*'s turret, just as hers did from our sloping sides. For two hours the cannonade continued without perceptible damage to either combatant." Then an accident occurred and *Virginia* ran aground.

Buchanan's haste to get *Virginia* into action meant that workers didn't have time to attach iron plates below its waterline. When it ran aground, *Virginia*'s soft underbelly was exposed. Had the *Monitor* known this, it could have easily sunk the *Virginia*. But *Virginia* broke free from the mud before the *Monitor*'s crew noticed its trouble. Gliding by the *Monitor*, *Virginia* fired on the *Minnesota*. *Monitor* hurried to the rescue. The battle of the ironclads that ensued carried away the *Monitor*'s steering gear, damaged the pilothouse and blinded Captain John Lorimer Worden, who was replaced by Lieutenant Samuel Dana Green as the engagement with the *Virginia* continued. The *Minnesota* was about to give up ship until its crew saw the *Virginia* turn toward Norfolk. *Virginia* broke off its attack on the *Monitor* until its underside iron plates could be put on.

About three weeks after the *Virginia*'s two-day engagement in Hampton Roads, the ironclad was ready to return to battle, but the *Monitor*—reinforced by two additional ironclads, USSs *Galena* and *Naugatuck*, and every available vessel of the United States Navy—was under strict orders from Washington to refuse *Virginia*'s challenge. Washington's strategy was to blockade *Virginia* in the Elizabeth River. Commodore Josiah Tattnall relieved Buchanan in command. Tattnall commanded the *Virginia* only forty-five days. Major General Benjamin Huger's Confederate troops abandoned Norfolk and Portsmouth in May 1862. *Virginia*'s draft was too deep to follow Huger up the James River. The decision was made to take *Virginia* to the bight of Craney Island and set it on fire rather than risk its capture. This was done on May 11, 1862. At just after half-past four in the morning, the ironclad's magazine exploded, its low, deep, mournful boom carrying over the water before *Virginia* sank to the river bottom. But the *Virginia* wasn't the only casualty of Huger's withdrawal. Confederate General Joseph Eggleston Johnston ordered his forces to abandon and destroy the Gosport Navy Yard on May 10. After this was done, Gosport once again lay in ruins.

When United States Navy Commodore John William Turk Livingston assumed command of the navy yard on May 20, 1862, he rechristened it the United States Navy Yard, Norfolk, Virginia, referred to herein as the Norfolk Navy Yard. Finding only the officers' quarters intact, he reported in early June to Joseph Smith, chief of the navy's Yard and Docks Bureau, that marines assigned to protect the base were housed in tents because "there are no buildings in this yard suitable to house them, but the two buildings composing the first lieutenant's and master's houses." Since Livingston's first priority was to restore yard operations, fire-damaged buildings would have to wait. The war raged on, brother against brother, yet somehow the beating heart of the navy's presence in Hampton Roads, the Norfolk Navy Yard, would survive it and triumph in the years to come.

Confederate troops occupied Yorktown and Gloucester Point, directly across the York River, at the beginning of the Civil War. But the South's hold on both sides of the river crumbled in the spring of 1862. With insufficient wharf space at Fort Monroe to land large numbers of troops and supplies, Federal forces used Ship Point, closer to Yorktown. Still not enough, Union Major General George Brinton McClellan's troops laid siege to Yorktown from April 5 to May 4, 1862, which forced the Confederates out of Yorktown and Gloucester Point. The landing at Yorktown belonged to the Federals when this picture was taken in the spring of 1862. *Courtesy of the Library of Congress Prints and Photographs Division.*

Brigadier General John Bankhead Magruder's Confederate troops erected a water battery at Yorktown, which they named for him, at the start of the Civil War. The eight-inch Columbiads and parapet overlooked the York River. Yorktown served as Magruder's headquarters until May 1862, when he withdrew his forces. By the time this picture was taken that June, at the peak of the Peninsular Campaign, Federal transports carrying troops and supplies populated the river, and Union soldiers posed on the parapet for George N. Barnard to take their picture. *Courtesy of the Library of Congress Prints and Photographs Division.*

The United States auxiliary screw steam frigate *Merrimack*, shown here off the entrance to New York Harbor, mounted sixty guns. *Merrimack* was built at Boston Navy Yard and commissioned February 20, 1856. After leaving Boston, it cruised the West Indies and European waters in 1856–57. Following minor repairs, it set sail in October 1857 as flagship of the Pacific Squadron, cruising the Pacific coasts of South and Central America until November 1859. Returning east, *Merrimack* was decommissioned at Norfolk, Virginia, February 16, 1860. On April 20, 1861, in the confusion following the outbreak of the Civil War, retiring Union forces burned *Merrimack* to the waterline and sank it to preclude capture by the Virginia militia. *Courtesy of the Library of Congress Prints and Photographs Division.*

Franklin Buchanan had over forty-five years of service to the United States Navy prior to the Civil War. From 1845 to 1847, he had served as the first superintendent of the United States Naval Academy. From 1859 to 1861, Captain Buchanan was commandant of the Washington Navy Yard. But when the war broke out, he chose the Confederacy. He was captain of the CSS *Virginia*, participating in March 8, 1862 action but not the *Virginia*'s engagement with the Union ironclad *Monitor*. He'd been wounded in action against the USS *Congress*, and Lieutenant Catesby ap Roger Jones took command. Confederate States Navy Commodore Buchanan is shown here during the war. *Courtesy of the Library of Congress Prints and Photographs Division*.

Union troops observed what was arguably the most important battle of the Civil War between the USS *Monitor* and CSS *Virginia*, née *Merrimack*, on March 9, 1862, perhaps shocked at the remarkable firepower of the world's first ironclads. The *Monitor* had moved past Old Point Comfort under cover of darkness, slipping into the Hampton Roads anchorage covered by the USS *Minnesota* and its accompanying squadron. During the fight that ensued, *Minnesota* (left) was struck below the waterline by a volley from the *Virginia* as the Confederate ironclad moved into position to engage the *Monitor*. Wounded men from the USSs *Minnesota* and *Congress* limped to shore by any means possible. Despite damage to both Federal frigates, they continued to fire on *Virginia*. This rendering of the battle by Kurz and Allen dates to 1889. *Courtesy of the Library of Congress Prints and Photographs Division.*

Rear Admiral John Lorimer Worden, shown here between 1872 and 1880, was commander of the USS *Monitor* when it engaged the CSS *Virginia* at Hampton Roads. Worden did not become a flag officer until 1872, when he was promoted to rear admiral; thus, the photograph could not have been taken before that date. He had just completed a five-year stint as commandant of the United States Naval Academy. *Courtesy of the Brady-Handy Photograph Collection, Library of Congress Prints and Photographs Division.*

With no deep draft available for inland escape and unable to put to open sea, the world's first ironclad was destroyed by its crew just above Craney Island on May 11, 1862, to avoid capture by the Union. This hand-colored lithograph of the *Virginia*'s destruction was published by Currier & Ives, of the period. *Courtesy of the Library of Congress Prints and Photographs Division.*

CSS *Virginia* did not emerge unscathed from its two-day battle with the Federal fleet and the USS *Monitor*, March 8–9, 1862, at Hampton Roads. The Southern ironclad's riddled stack, described as "shot away," limited its modest mobility and speed. But it also had other problems. *Virginia* had also lost the use of two of its large guns, several armor plates were loose and its ram had been lost in USS *Cumberland*. The battered smokestack of the CSS *Virginia* was photographed at an unknown location, though the backdrop of the picture suggests the Norfolk Navy Yard, between 1862 and 1865. *Courtesy of the Library of Congress Prints and Photographs Division.*

The battered flag of the CSS *Virginia*, the world's first ironclad, was recovered after its destruction at Craney Island in May 1862. This flag was the First Confederate Navy Ensign, in use from 1861 to 1863, and consists of a circle of seven five-pointed white stars against a field of medium blue in the corner and two red bars separated by a white bar in the center. It was flown aft aboard all Confederate warships and appears in nearly all lithographs of the *Virginia* in combat and in port. The flag was photographed circa 1910. *Courtesy of the Library of Congress Prints and Photographs Division.*

James F. Gibson, arguably the least known of Mathew Brady's Civil War photographers, took this picture of twelve of the USS *Monitor*'s officers posed in front of its turret on July 9, 1862. Gibson's James River backdrop was only a short distance upriver from Hampton Roads. *Courtesy of the Library of Congress Prints and Photographs Division.*

There are no known photographs that show a broadside or complete view of the USS *Monitor*. But there are several of its crew. James F. Gibson took this photograph of the ironclad's sailors relaxing on its deck on July 9, 1862; it had been sent up the James River from Hampton Roads, where months before *Monitor* had engaged the CSS *Virginia*. *Courtesy of the Library of Congress Prints and Photographs Division.*

James Gibson took this picture of two officers surveying the deck and turret of the ironclad USS *Monitor* on the James River on July 9, 1862. The deck plate to the right of them was slightly loosened by the CSS *Virginia*, which had tried to ram the ironclad during their engagement in Hampton Roads. *Courtesy of the Library of Congress Prints and Photographs Division.*

The USS *Monitor*'s sailors were preparing a meal on the large cookstove (left) when James Gibson took this picture, also on July 9, 1862. *Courtesy of the Library of Congress Prints and Photographs Division.*

The side-wheel, steam-powered gunboat USS *Hunchback* was primarily used to patrol the coastal reaches of southeastern Virginia but also saw action in northeastern North Carolina sounds. The Union navy acquired this vessel from a civilian operator on December 16, 1861, and commissioned the ferry-turned-gunboat on January 3, 1862. *Hunchback* went back to ferrying civilian passengers after the navy decommissioned it on June 12, 1865. Mathew Brady took this picture of *Hunchback*'s officers and crew. *Courtesy of the National Archives and Records Administration.*

A boatswain's mate was photographed piping in front of a large cannon on the deck of an unidentified United States Navy warship during the Civil War. *Courtesy of the Library of Congress Prints and Photographs Division.*

Mathew Brady photographed sailors and marines aboard the Union side-wheel steamer USS *Mendota* sometime in 1864. *Mendota* was a latecomer to the war. It was commissioned on May 2, 1864, Commander Edward Tattnall Nichols in command, and decommissioned on May 12, 1865. For most of its service, *Mendota* was used as a bombardment gunboat but also as a blockade ship. During its last two months of service, *Mendota* directed ship movements at Hampton Roads and also the mouth of the Delaware River. *Courtesy of the National Archives and Records Administration.*

The Gosport Navy Yard, renamed the Norfolk Navy Yard in 1862, was set on fire twice during the Civil War. When Virginia joined the Confederate States of America in April 1861, Gosport's Federal commander, anticipating that the Confederacy would seize the yard, ordered his sailors to torch it. As they evacuated on the night of April 20, 1861, his sailors set fire to buildings, equipment and stores at the yard and either burned or scuttled eleven ships at their Elizabeth River mooring. They also made an unsuccessful attempt to blow up the dry dock, which was the first ever built in the United States. It was only a matter of months before the shipyard was set ablaze again, this time on May 10, 1862, when the Confederate States Navy evacuated Gosport. Federal forces reoccupied the shipyard immediately and held control of it until the end of the war. The ruins of the yard were photographed in December 1864 by James Gardner. *Courtesy of the Library of Congress Prints and Photographs Division.*

John Driscoll, a Union veteran of the fight between the USS *Monitor* and CSS *Virginia*, points to the spot in Hampton Roads where the battle occurred in March 1862. The photograph was taken in 1916. *Courtesy of the Harris and Ewing Collection, Library of Congress Prints and Photographs Division.*

After the Confederacy evacuated Norfolk in May 1862, the Hampton Roads anchorage filled with Union naval forces waiting to enter Norfolk waters, including the ammunition schooners shown here, which by December 1864, when this picture was taken off Fort Norfolk, moved cargo up and down the Elizabeth River. Fort Norfolk was an ammunition store for the Union army; thus, the vessels were a frequent sight in proximity to the fort's wharf. *Courtesy of the Library of Congress Prints and Photographs Division.*

Rear Admiral David Dixon Porter (the bearded man, center, facing the photographer) and his staff were photographed aboard the admiral's flagship, USS *Malvern*, at Hampton Roads in December 1864. At the time this picture was taken, Porter was in command of the North Atlantic Blockading Squadron. This highly decorated hero of the Civil War attained the rank of admiral and became the naval service's senior officer in the post–Civil War years. He died on February 13, 1891, at the age of seventy-seven. *Courtesy of the Library of Congress Prints and Photographs Division.*

United States Navy officers relaxed on the deck of an unidentified warship, circa 1865.
Courtesy of the Library of Congress Prints and Photographs Division.

The 642-ton iron-hulled side-wheel gunboat USS *Fort Donelson* was built in 1860 at Glasgow, Scotland, as the commercial steamer *Giraffe*. In 1862, it became the Confederate blockade runner *Robert E. Lee* and, during the next year, successfully breached the Federal blockade of the South more than twenty times. While attempting to reach Wilmington, North Carolina, on November 9, 1863, it was captured by the USSs *James Adger* and *Iron Age*. The *Fort Donelson* was anchored in the Elizabeth River when this picture was taken in December 1864. *Courtesy of the Library of Congress Prints and Photographs Division.*

The 1,477-ton burden iron-hulled side-wheel gunboat USS *Malvern* was photographed off Norfolk, Virginia, in December 1864. *Malvern* was built in 1860 as the commercial steamship *William G. Hewes*. For a brief time, it was a Confederate blockade runner named *Ella and Annie*. After the Union navy captured the gunboat on November 9, 1863, trying to gain access to the port of Wilmington, North Carolina, it was converted and eventually commissioned in February 1864 as the *Malvern*. Shortly thereafter, it was named the flagship of the North Atlantic Blockading Squadron. In early April 1865, *Malvern* transported President Abraham Lincoln up the James River to visit Richmond, Virginia, former capital of the Confederacy. *Courtesy of the Library of Congress Prints and Photographs Division.*

Vice Admiral David Farragut, foster brother of Rear Admiral David Dixon Porter, had been chosen to lead Union naval forces, part of a joint land-sea expedition, against the Confederate stronghold Fort Fisher at the mouth of North Carolina's Cape Fear River, but he was too ill to do so. Porter transferred from his command of the North Atlantic Blockading Squadron and took Farragut's place. The fleet rendezvoused at Hampton Roads (shown here) in early December 1864. There were two attacks against Fort Fisher, the first December 24–27, 1864, and the second January 12–15, 1865. The second attack left the Union victorious. Porter's force consisted of thirty-seven ships, five of them monitors towed down from Fort Monroe, and a reserve force of nineteen vessels. *Courtesy of the Library of Congress Prints and Photographs Division.*

The USS *Santiago de Cuba* was a wooden, brigantine-rigged, side-wheel steamer built in 1861 at Brooklyn, New York, and bought by the navy that September. The *Santiago de Cuba* was photographed in Hampton Roads off Fort Monroe in mid-January 1865. The steamer had just delivered wounded to Norfolk, Virginia, from the bloody Union defeat of Confederate forces at Fort Fisher, in the vicinity of Wilmington, North Carolina. *Courtesy of the Library of Congress Prints and Photographs Division.*

Chapter 3

Iron Men, Steel Ships

The United States Navy, with more warships in service than prewar years, experienced an increased demand for shore facilities after the Civil War. But what it soon discovered was a shore establishment far less capable than navy leadership had hoped. Extensive wartime damage to the Norfolk and Pensacola Navy Yards, coupled with the closing of the shipyard at Memphis, Tennessee, disadvantaged the postwar fleet. The 1865 annual report to the secretary of war identified the lack of space at navy shore facilities as hampering the ability of the fleet to operate effectively. Exacerbating the problem was the rise of ironclad technology. All of the existing navy yards were designed to build and maintain a wooden fleet. The national debt incurred by the prosecution of the Civil War restrained Congress from appropriating funds to improve navy facilities. In 1874, the United States Senate Committee on Naval Affairs was asked by Congress to study the feasibility of naval yard closures. The committee came back with a recommendation to expand the Norfolk yard, citing its strategic location. Nine years later, in 1883, a similar committee was convened by Congress and observed that while the Norfolk Navy Yard had the capability to build and repair wood warships of all sizes, it was unable to construct, or even dry-dock, the new iron-hulled *Chicago*-class vessels. This shortcoming didn't spell the yard's closure.

The Norfolk Navy Yard's strategic location made it, even then, the most important naval shipyard on the Atlantic Coast. Navy Commander Edward Phelps Lull, in his *History of the United States Navy Yard at Gosport, Virginia*, published in 1874, wrote:

No navy yard belonging to the United States is from its geographical position more important than that of Gosport, Virginia. Located near enough to the entrance of Chesapeake Bay to be easily accessible, it is, at the same time, in a position readily defended from attacks either by land or by water, and one, as has been repeatedly shown, which can be held by a small force against a very largely superior one. There is in the vicinity an abundant supply of timber and other material, while the close proximity of a populous city secures to it the command of all the skilled labor that can be required. Such is the mildness of the climate that work of all sorts can be carried on at all seasons of the year without interruption. Hampton Roads, the outer harbor, is an excellent point of rendezvous for a fleet or squadron.

Lull went on to remark that a glance at the map would demonstrate the great importance of a naval station in the vicinity of the yard. "The Chesapeake, with its navigable tributaries, penetrates into the heart of several of the richest states in the Union, reaching to the national capitol," he continued. "A foothold in its waters would, therefore, be of the utmost strategic importance to an invading enemy, and would probably be one of the earliest objects sought by them, as past history has fully shown. The width of the entrance of the bay is so great that it would be impossible to defend it except by a naval force, which should have a repairing, coaling and victualing station as near at hand as possible consistent with entire defensibility for itself, with a reasonably secure outer harbor, large enough for the necessary maneuvers of a squadron in getting under way and forming. All of these conditions are admirably filled by the location of the Gosport yard." But even Lull's words didn't move Washington to action, at least not right away.

The United States made its greatest post–Civil War strides toward modernization of its fleet and naval shore facilities during the administration of President Chester Arthur, in office from September 19, 1881, to March 4, 1885. As he came into office, Arthur nominated New Hampshire lawyer William Eaton Chandler to be his secretary of the navy. He did so knowing Chandler's desire to put an end to the practice of repairing wooden-hulled warships, which were no match for the ordnance employed during and after the Civil War. The CSS *Virginia*'s demonstration of firepower at the Battle of Hampton Roads hadn't been ignored. Arthur wanted a modern navy, and the only way to get it was to stock the Navy Department with men who could get the job done. Chandler almost immediately sought to streamline and reorganize the sea service's outmoded navy yard establishment, a measure which met with resistance from those with one foot in the sailing navy. Chandler, who has been called the father of the modern navy, wrote in his 1883 annual report that "in order to be prepared, not merely by the potentiality of our immense resources, but also by an actual armament, to assert at all times our natural, justifiable, and necessary ascendancy in the affairs of the American hemisphere, we unquestionably need vessels in such numbers as fully to keep alive the knowledge of war, and of such a kind that it shall be a knowledge of modern war; capable, on brief notice, of being expanded into invincible squadrons." But the old navy establishment wasn't quick to embrace an iron-hulled warship. Progress was slow in coming, and so was the money.

Congress authorized only two steel ships in August 1882 and no money for their construction. This did not deter Chandler. He pressed forward, standing up the navy's Second Advisory Board, chaired by Rear Admiral Robert Shufeldt, in the fall of 1882. Shufeldt understood the mindset of his predecessors and colleagues, men who moved in measured steps rather than giant leaps. Thus, the Shufeldt board moved in kind, recommending only four steel ships be built in the first phase of modernization. Congress agreed, making slight changes to Shufeldt's proposal. On March 3, 1883, $1.3 million was appropriated to construct three steel cruisers and one gunboat/dispatch boat. These four steel ships have been dubbed the "ABCD" ships after the first letter of each warship's name: *Atlanta, Boston, Chicago*—all protected cruisers—and *Dolphin*, the gunboat/dispatch boat. Though the cruisers were armored with steel plate to cover their armament and mechanical spaces, they bore only a thin layer of steel to the hull. And they also compromised in another, obvious, respect: though each of them was capable of getting underway via coal-fired steam power, all had been fitted with sails with which they were expected to operate under normal cruising conditions.

Early efforts by Arthur, Chandler and Shufeldt paid greater dividends in the years to come. Naval historians have repeatedly observed that the path to the navy's first steel warship pointed to the significant deterioration of the sea service in the post–Civil War years, most especially its aging shore establishment. Modern ships couldn't be built in navy yards that hadn't kept pace with new technology and organization. Thus, the navy began to rely on a familiar roster of private shipbuilders to prepare drawings, specifications and construction of the new navy. This marriage of the navy to the private shipbuilding industry, birthed in the mid-nineteenth century, paved the way for the vast military industrial complex that took off during the height of the steel navy period. Private industry caught on quickly and, by the end of the 1880s, had learned to refine and improve navy technology and hardware, providing a better product than the navy could have, just then, ever produced on its own. Evidence of this emerged with the construction of the American Battle Fleet's bigger, better and faster battleships, cruisers, destroyers, auxiliaries and, later, aircraft carriers, built both in navy and private yards in years that followed.

As the result of Arthur's early fleet modernization initiatives, Norfolk Navy Yard received money for significant improvements. An electrical fire-alarm system was fitted at the navy yard in 1886, and in 1888, a new telephone system was installed, followed the next year by the first use of a railroad car in the yard, which also completed a second dry dock. As war with Spain approached, wood and canvas gave way to steel and steam. The navy yard at Norfolk built two of the first ships of the modern navy: the steel-sheathed USS *Raleigh* (C-8), a protected cruiser, and the steel-hulled USS *Texas*, a second-class battleship, both launched in 1892. The *Raleigh* was the first ship of the new navy to be completely built by the United States government, and the *Texas* was the navy's first battleship, but it was also powered exclusively by steam. The launching of the *Raleigh* corresponded with the International Columbian Naval Rendezvous in Hampton Roads, celebrating the 400th anniversary of European awareness of the Americas.

The mission of the Norfolk Navy Yard prior to the Spanish-American War had been to build, supply and maintain the United States fleet. Both the *Raleigh* and *Texas*, the progeny of the Norfolk yard, also gave it fame. Both warships garnered worldwide attention during the Spanish-American War, the *Texas* at Santiago, where, with the assistance of USS *Massachusetts* (BB-2), it sank the *Reina Mercedes*. The *Raleigh* brought home its reputation from its participation in the thickest of the fight at the Battle of Manila Bay. The captured *Reina Mercedes* was brought to the United States Navy Yard Norfolk on May 27, 1899, as a prize of war. On that day, the riverbanks leading to the yard were lined with thousands of onlookers anxious to see *Texas*'s handiwork. The twenty-two tugs that escorted the *Reina Mercedes* into the mainstem of the Elizabeth River had plenty of room to maneuver as they approached Hospital Point. Four hundred feet had been removed from the point to facilitate the transit of larger navy warships.

After the Spanish-American War, the traditional role of naval yards was expanded and altered by the demands of the steel navy. At Norfolk, land based schools for sailors were established. Down the waterfront from the hospital, the Norfolk yard's third dry dock was begun in 1903 and completed in 1911. Constructed of granite and concrete, this dock was only one of many new shipbuilding facilities, necessitating expansion to the south and west. Rear Admiral Purnell Harrington, commander of the yard, complained to the Board of Navy Yard Plans in October 1904 that the functions housed in the yard were ill organized and scattered throughout the base. To support his claim that many structures on the yard did not support the new navy's steel-clad warships, Harrington conducted a building survey that provided a description of each building's operational function. On the date of the assessment, October 14, 1904, he identified Building 28 as housing the mast construction division of a sail-powered navy. Harrington recommended reorganization; he got it. From Harrington's practical initiatives to Chandler's sweeping modernization of the fleet, a new navy emerged.

The International Columbian Naval Rendezvous held April 17–24, 1893, at Hampton Roads, Virginia, was expected to be the greatest international gathering of warships since Queen Victoria's 1887 Golden Jubilee. Thirty-eight warships from ten countries gathered in Hampton Roads as the first of several celebrations leading up to the Chicago Columbian Exposition. The rendezvous solidified Hampton Roads's importance to the American navy, which moored fourteen of its newest warships off Old Point Comfort under the command of Rear Admiral Bancroft Gherardi. Sailors ran liberty boats, shown here, that carried American and foreign sailors and civilians back and forth from ship to shore. *Courtesy of the author.*

Begun in 1886 by industrialist Collis Potter Huntington, Newport News Shipbuilding (NNS) and Dry Dock Company delivered its first ships to the United States Navy—the USSs *Nashville*, *Wilmington* and *Helena*—in 1897. Between 1907 and 1923, NNS built six of the navy's twenty-two total battleships: the *Delaware*, *Texas*, *Pennsylvania*, *Mississippi*, *Maryland* and *West Virginia*. When President Theodore Roosevelt sent the Great White Fleet around the world in 1907, seven of the sixteen battleships he dispatched from Hampton Roads had been built by NNS. Between 1918 and 1920, the yard delivered twenty-five destroyers, and shortly thereafter it began building aircraft carriers. NNS built the first keel-up aircraft carrier, the USS *Ranger* (CV-4), launched on February 25, 1933, and it went on to build *Yorktown* (CV-5) and *Enterprise* (CV-6). *Courtesy of the Library of Congress Prints and Photographs Division.*

Prior to its purchase by Northrop Grumman in 2001, Newport News Shipbuilding was the largest privately owned shipyard in the United States; it remains one of only two shipyards in the country that builds and services all types of nuclear-powered submarines and is the only yard that builds the nation's aircraft carriers. This Newport News Shipbuilding machine shop, shown as it appeared in 1905, was the largest of its kind in the United States at that time. *Courtesy of the Library of Congress Prints and Photographs Division.*

USS *Iowa*, Coastal Battleship No. 4 and later BB-4, was unique in that it did not belong to a specific ship class. Commissioned on June 16, 1897, *Iowa* saw extensive action in the Spanish-American War under the command of the legendary William Thomas Sampson, then a captain. After the war, it was assigned to the United States Atlantic Fleet but was placed in reserve on July 6, 1907, and decommissioned on July 23, 1908. This photograph of an inspection aboard *Iowa* was taken in 1906. *Iowa* was recommissioned on April 28, 1917, and sent to Hampton Roads, where it remained for the rest of World War I guarding the Chesapeake Bay and training sailors for duty aboard other ships. *Iowa* returned to full active duty in April 1922 to take part in gunfire exercises in Hampton Roads; it was sunk as a bombing target in 1923. *Courtesy of the Library of Congress Prints and Photographs Division.*

USS *Kentucky* (BB-6), a *Kearsarge*-class battleship launched on March 24, 1898, by Newport News Shipbuilding, was sponsored by Christine Bradley, daughter of Kentucky governor William Bradley, and commissioned on May 16, 1900, Captain Colby M. Chester in command. The guns and gunners of the *Kentucky* are shown on the face of this Raphael Tuck and Sons Postcard Series No. 2326 titled "U.S. Navy," published circa 1905. *Kentucky* visited Norfolk on April 15, 1907, during the Jamestown Exposition and returned again that December to join the Great White Fleet's world cruise. *Courtesy of the author*.

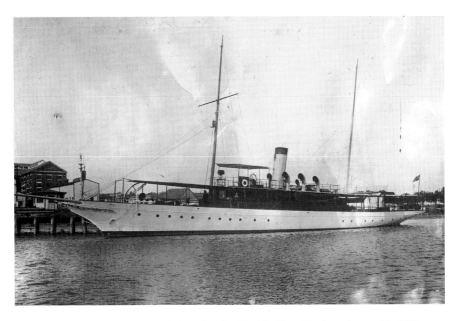

The USS *Sylph* (PY-5) was commissioned at the Norfolk Navy Yard on August 18, 1898, and used as a presidential yacht until it was decommissioned on April 27, 1929. President William McKinley was the first to use it. In 1902, *Sylph* began alternating first with the gunboat USS *Dolphin* (PG-24) and then USS *Mayflower* (PY-1) as the president's waterborne transportation. *Courtesy of the George Grantham Bain Collection, Library of Congress Prints and Photographs Division.*

USS *Solace*, shown here on December 10, 1916, in Hampton Roads, was originally built in 1896 and 1897 by Newport News Shipbuilding and operated as the SS *Creole* by the Cromwell Steamship Lines. But on April 7, 1898, *Creole* was acquired by the United States Navy and renamed *Solace*. *Solace* was converted into a hospital ship, the first United States Navy ship to fly the Geneva Red Cross flag. *Solace* was commissioned on April 14, 1898, and, after more than two decades of service, was decommissioned on July 20, 1921, and struck from the Navy Vessel Register on August 6, 1930. *Courtesy of the Library of Congress Prints and Photographs Division.*

The auxiliary screw steamer USS *Buffalo* (later AD-8) was originally built in 1892 at Newport News Shipbuilding and Drydock Company as *El Cid*. Six months later, it was sold to Brazil and named *Nicheroy*. But it was purchased from Brazil by the United States Navy on July 11, 1898, and renamed *Buffalo*. Commander Joseph Newton Hemphill, shown here, was made commanding officer of the United States dynamite gunboat *Buffalo* on September 22, 1898. This cabinet card was conveyed directly from Hemphill to an unknown recipient on July 1, 1898, at the New York Navy Yard, where *Buffalo* was fitted out for deployment. Hemphill died in 1931 in Washington, D.C., at age eighty-three. *Courtesy of the author.*

Workers in this Newport News Shipbuilding machine shop were photographed punching single bars for the USS *Illinois* (BB-7), lead ship of its class, in early 1898. *Illinois* was laid down on February 10, 1897, launched October 4, 1898, and commissioned September 16, 1901. *Courtesy of the Library of Congress Prints and Photographs Division.*

The protected cruiser USS *Detroit* (C-10) was launched October 28, 1891, by Columbian Iron Works, Baltimore, Maryland, and commissioned July 20, 1893, with Commander Willard Herbert Brownson in command. This was the third ship to be named for Detroit, Michigan. *Detroit* steamed from Norfolk on October 5, 1893, for Rio de Janeiro, Brazil, where it laid anchor in the harbor to protect American citizens and interests during revolutionary disturbances in that country. The cruiser returned to Norfolk on April 24, 1894. *Detroit* departed Norfolk again that October 16 to serve on the Asiatic Station for two years, cruising the Chinese coast and visiting ports in Japan and Korea, ultimately returning to New York City on May 17, 1897. This image of the *Detroit* was produced on a cabinet card by Yee Chun of Hong Kong. *Courtesy of the author.*

During *Detroit*'s deployment to the Far East, this sailor had his picture taken by Pun Lun of Hong Kong. *Courtesy of the author.*

76

Hampton Roads

USS *Texas* was the United States Navy's first battleship. Authorized by Congress on August 3, 1886, its keel was laid at Norfolk Navy Yard on June 1, 1889, and it was launched June 28, 1892. *Texas* was not commissioned until August 15, 1895. Sailors aboard *Texas* called it an unlucky ship, nicknaming it "Old Hoodoo" after a series of accidents and incidents that damaged the ship. Certainly, *Texas* was poorly designed; its armament was mounted *en echelon*, a poor design that limited its ability to fire broadside. Assigned to the North Atlantic Squadron, it cruised the East Coast, working extensively out of Hampton Roads. *Texas* is shown here with the *Whisper*, a riverboat, during a 1900 visit to New Orleans. *Courtesy of the Library of Congress Prints and Photographs Division.*

After the Spanish-American War, *Texas* was put out of commission in 1901 for repairs at Norfolk Navy Yard but recommissioned on November 3, 1902. *Texas* was the flagship of the Coast Squadron in 1905, once again resuming patrol of the East Coast. But *Texas*'s life was short-lived; its name was changed to *San Marcos* on February 15, 1911, to permit the name "Texas" to be assigned to a new battleship soon under construction at Newport News Shipbuilding. On October 10, 1911, it was stricken from the Naval Vessel Register, and it was later sunk in Tangier Sound in the Chesapeake Bay during target practice. This photograph, taken in 1900, shows the *Texas*'s mascots: a puppy sitting in the barrel of a thirteen-inch gun and a kitten on top. *Courtesy of the Library of Congress Prints and Photographs Division.*

The United States gunboat *Nashville* (PG-7) was laid down on August 9, 1894, at Newport News Shipbuilding, launched on October 19, 1895, and commissioned August 19, 1897, Commander Washburn Maynard in command. *Nashville* was sent to the Caribbean after the USS *Maine* (ACR-1) was destroyed in Havana Harbor on February 15, 1898; it fired the first shot in America's war with Spain and captured four Spanish ships between April 22 and July 26. *Nashville* also assisted in cutting the undersea telegraph cable off Cienfuegos, in which many of its sailors and marines earned Medals of Honor. The fabled gunboat is pictured here at the Norfolk Navy Yard on January 8, 1898. *Courtesy of the author.*

The *Arkansas*-class monitor USS *Florida* (BM-9) was launched on November 30, 1901, and commissioned on June 18, 1903. *Florida* served with the Coast Squadron and as a training ship before being renamed *Tallahassee* on July 1, 1908, to allow for the name "Florida" to be assigned to a new battleship. *Tallahassee* was placed in reserve commission on August 1, 1910, and used for ordnance experimentation and in the Panama Canal Zone and Hampton Roads as a submarine tender. The monitor is shown here with two *K*-class submarines, *K-5* (SS-36) and *K-6* (SS-37), on December 10, 1916, at Hampton Roads. *K-5* and *K-6* frequently operated in Hampton Roads and the Chesapeake Bay. *Courtesy of the Library of Congress Prints and Photographs Division.*

USS *Paducah*, Gunboat No. 18, was launched on October 11, 1904, and commissioned September 2, 1905. *Paducah* joined the Caribbean Squadron in early 1906 to protect American lives and interests, patrolling Caribbean and Central and South American waters. Sailors of the *Paducah* also visited numerous Central and South American cities, where they likely picked up their mascot, a black-headed spider monkey, shown here on this real picture postcard mailed November 26, 1908, from Portsmouth, New Hampshire. From the aftermath of the Veracruz incident through the summer of 1914, *Paducah* patrolled Mexican waters before returning to its normal Caribbean and, later, East Coast operations. *Courtesy of the author.*

The *New York*–class battleship USS *Texas*'s (BB-35) keel was laid down at Newport News Shipbuilding on April 17, 1911. *Texas* was still in prelaunch construction when this picture was taken. *Courtesy of the Library of Congress Prints and Photographs Division.*

A large crowd gathered for the launching of the USS *Texas* (BB-35) on May 18, 1912, at Newport News Shipbuilding. *Courtesy of the Library of Congress Prints and Photographs Division.*

Claudia Lyon, *Texas*'s sponsor, and Secretary of the Navy George von Lengerke Meyer were photographed on the christening platform on *Texas*'s launch day, May 18, 1912. Claudia was the daughter of Colonel Cecil Lyon, Republican national committeeman from Texas. Meyer was President William Howard Taft's secretary of the navy from 1909 to 1913. *Courtesy of the Library of Congress Prints and Photographs Division.*

Texas slipped down the ways and into Hampton Roads as thousands watched on May 18, 1912. Soon after its commissioning on March 12, 1914, USS *Texas* saw action in Mexican waters following the "Tampico Incident" and made numerous sorties into the North Sea during World War I. When the United States formally entered World War II in 1941, *Texas* took on the role of escorting war convoys across the Atlantic and later shelled Axis-held beaches for the North African campaign and the Normandy landings before being transferred to the Pacific Theater late in 1944 to provide naval gunfire support during the Battles of Iwo Jima and Okinawa. *Texas* earned a total of five battle stars for service in World War II and was decommissioned in 1948; it is presently a museum ship near Houston, Texas. *Courtesy of the Library of Congress Prints and Photographs Division.*

Chapter 4

When the Fleet Went Around the World

The grandest naval expedition undertaken by the United States in the early twentieth century assembled in Hampton Roads in December 1907, the final curtain call of the Jamestown Exposition, the tercentennial celebration of the first permanent English settlement in America. President Theodore Roosevelt's Great White Fleet came to symbolize America's world-power status and the years invested to build a navy greater than any other nation, even if that fleet was outmoded before it ever steamed out of the Chesapeake Bay. At that time, the American Battle Fleet was arguably not only the greatest fighting force on the high seas but also one that had made great strides in proficiency and efficiency. The fleet's fourteen-month circumnavigation of the world was the longest cruise ever made by the fleet of any nation. But it was also a Roosevelt calculated risk that paid for itself in social capital and global recognition for decades to come.

After Japan defeated the Imperial Russian Navy in the 1904–1905 Russo-Japanese War, the West detected a new threat in the Far East. Japan's emerging military strength could potentially reach beyond the waters of the eastern hemisphere, and this fact was not ignored by Roosevelt. As 1906 came and went, Roosevelt was eager to demonstrate to Japan's emperor that the American Battle Fleet wouldn't be such an easy target. The British Royal Navy, though America's elder on the high seas, had little interest in Japan. Great Britain had enough trouble with its own commonwealth and colonial protectorates, problems that far outweighed proving its naval superiority to an emerging military power in the East. Besides, in the British admiralty's opinion, there was no clear sign, not just then, that war with Japan was on the horizon; thus, its resources were better spent battling unrest in Britain's extant territories. Roosevelt was on his own. Though the president never announced the true objective of the fleet's circumnavigation of the world, it was Japan. The Japanese provided elaborate exhibitory to the exposition and also gifted the stone bridge over the Grand Basin. But Tokyo was quick to express disappointment that the use of Japanese cabin boys would soon be terminated on American naval vessels as their enlistments ended. Newspapers took their termination as a sign that the American Battle Fleet was preparing for war with Japan, though this was not true, not then. Roosevelt's battle fleet had no trouble finding young men to man its ships. The fleet had come into its own, a force to be reckoned with on the high seas.

The American Battle Fleet was designated in December 1907 in preparation for its December 16 departure from Hampton Roads. The fleet was made up of two squadrons, sixteen battleships in all, moored in the waters in view of crowds gathered for the close of the Jamestown Exposition. The first squadron included the battleships USSs *Connecticut* (BB-18), *Maine* (BB-10), *Louisiana* (BB-19), *Missouri* (BB-11), *Virginia* (BB-13), *Rhode Island* (BB-17), *New Jersey* (BB-16) and *Georgia* (BB-15), and the second was composed of the USSs *Alabama* (BB-8), *Illinois* (BB-7), *Kentucky* (BB-6), *Kearsarge* (BB-5), *Ohio* (BB-12), *Minnesota* (BB-22), *Iowa* (BB-4) and *Indiana* (BB-1). The big guns, which included additional battleships beyond the named sixteen, were escorted by five capital ships, five cruisers, six destroyers, torpedo boats and numerous auxiliary ships. The hulls of all American Battle Fleet ships were painted white, not the navy's haze gray, thus the nickname Great White Fleet. The two squadrons were divided into four divisions. The first formed around *Connecticut*, fleet commander Rear Admiral Robley Evans's flagship, and included *Louisiana*; and the new *Connecticut*-class battleships USSs *Kansas* (BB-21) and *Vermont* (BB-20). The second consisted of *Georgia*, *New Jersey*, *Rhode Island* and *Virginia*, but also the newly commissioned *Virginia*-class battleship *Nebraska* (BB-14), which didn't join the fleet until it reached San Francisco. The third included the *Minnesota*, *Ohio*, *Missouri* and *Maine*. And the fourth was made up of the *Alabama*, *Illinois*, *Kearsarge* and *Kentucky*, later joined in San Francisco by the *Illinois*-class battleship USS *Wisconsin* (BB-9). Seven of the sixteen battleships that set out from Hampton Roads on December 16 were built at Newport News Shipbuilding and Dry Dock Company: *Kearsarge*, *Kentucky*, *Illinois*, *Missouri*, *Virginia*, *Louisiana* and *Minnesota*.

On the eve of the fleet's departure, a grand ball was held at Old Point Comfort's Chamberlin Hotel, followed by a magnificent fireworks display and a line from Rear Admiral Evans that immortalized the Great White

Fleet to the American people. He declared his fleet ready for "a feast, a frolic, or a fight." Evans possessed all the character traits Roosevelt required: great tactician, charismatic leader and able administrator. The next morning, Evans was at the helm of the *Connecticut* as it steamed past an ebullient Roosevelt aboard the presidential yacht *Mayflower*. Newspapers reported in the days that followed that as the fleet passed out of Hampton Roads, a young woman leaned over to her escort and remarked, "Have we any navy left?" In reply, the young man said, "Oh, yes. There's the *Yankton*." But in truth, he was sorely misinformed. The *Yankton* left with the fleet, leaving only the old presidential yacht *Sylph* in port.

After the fleet's departure from Hampton Roads, Roosevelt still hadn't announced his intention of sending it around the world. He told reporters it was a practice cruise from Hampton Roads to South America. But once Evans's armada reached South America to replenish, it was clear that he wasn't taking the pride of America's fleet back to Hampton Roads. As the Great White Fleet transited to the Pacific, the rest of the world learned the president's true intention: to show Tokyo that America outranked and outgunned anything Japan could put to sea. But hidden in the president's bravado was his concern for the American shipbuilding industry, then in trouble. With shipbuilding appropriations tied up in Congress, Roosevelt came to the rescue the only way he knew how: by sending out the best of the fleet to show Congress the need for American domination on the high seas in the face of emerging navies in the East. Roosevelt got everything he wanted: he impressed America's legislators and Japan. In the end, both retreated. Roosevelt later observed that the most important service he rendered to peace during his presidency was "the voyage of the battle fleet around the world."

When USS *Connecticut* (BB-18) arrived at Hampton Roads on April 16, 1907, Rear Admiral Robley Dunglison Evans, the first commander in chief of the United States Atlantic Fleet, transferred his flag from USS *Maine* (BB-10) to *Connecticut*, thus making it the flagship of the fleet. Nine days later, President Theodore Roosevelt opened the Jamestown Exposition, and *Connecticut* was named the official host of all foreign visiting ships. *Connecticut*'s sailors and marines took part in events ashore, and foreign dignitaries, as well as the governors of Virginia and Rhode Island, were hosted aboard the ship on April 29. Evans closed the exposition on May 4 on *Connecticut*'s quarterdeck. On June 10, *Connecticut* joined the Presidential Fleet Review; three days later, the ship left for the first of two overhauls, both at the New York Navy Yard. After its final refit and its hull was painted white, *Connecticut* was suitable for use as flagship of the Great White Fleet. *Courtesy of the author.*

This Keystone View Company stereoview shows some of the great warships in Hampton Roads for the Jamestown Exposition's opening day, April 26, 1907. *Courtesy of the Library of Congress Prints and Photographs Division.*

Hampton Roads

The military parade that passed in front of the Auditorium Building on the opening day of the Jamestown Exposition, April 26, 1907, included sailors from the many American warships moored in Hampton Roads. *Courtesy of the Library of Congress Prints and Photographs Division.*

President Theodore Roosevelt (right) and Rear Admiral Robley "Fighting Bob" Evans were photographed on April 29, 1907, aboard the presidential yacht *Mayflower* (PY-1). *Courtesy of the Library of Congress Prints and Photographs Division.*

Connecticut left the New York Naval Yard on December 5, 1907, and arrived the next day in Hampton Roads, where the Great White Fleet assembled with *Connecticut* as its flagship. After an eight-day period known as Navy Farewell Week, during which departure parties were held for the fleet's sailors, all sixteen battleships took on full loads of coal, stores and ammunition and were ready to depart Hampton Roads. The battleship captains paid their respects to President Theodore Roosevelt on the *Mayflower* on December 16, and all the ships weighed anchor and departed at ten o'clock that morning. The fleet passed in review before the president as it traveled out of Hampton Roads and headed south past Cape Hatteras and out to sea. The *Connecticut* is shown here, on another occasion circa 1910, saluting the *Mayflower*. *Courtesy of the George Grantham Bain Collection, Library of Congress Prints and Photographs Division.*

The sixteen battleships of the Great White Fleet were photographed as they steamed past Old Point Comfort on December 16, 1907. *Courtesy of the author.*

The Great White Fleet returned to Hampton Roads on February 22, 1909, shown here. After a month passed, all of the battleships, destroyers and cruisers that had gone around the world were dispersed to naval shipyards for paintwork. All hulls were changed from white to the navy's traditional haze gray. *Courtesy of the author.*

Crowds and excursion boats gathered at Old Point Comfort, Fort Monroe, at the entrance to Hampton Roads to watch the Great White Fleet's February 22, 1909 return. *Courtesy of the George Grantham Bain Collection, Library of Congress Prints and Photographs Division.*

The presidential yacht *Mayflower* is shown off Hampton, Virginia, on February 22, 1909. *Courtesy of the George Grantham Bain Collection, Library of Congress Prints and Photographs Division.*

The night of its return to Hampton Roads, the Great White Fleet was illuminated off Old Point Comfort (shown here). *Courtesy of the George Grantham Bain Collection, Library of Congress Prints and Photographs Division.*

A sailor was photographed painting aboard the USS *Connecticut* (BB-18) in 1909. *Courtesy of the George Grantham Bain Collection, Library of Congress Prints and Photographs Division.*

Gunners gathered on the forecastle of the *Illinois*-class battleship *Wisconsin* (BB-9) on February 27, 1904. Commissioned three years earlier, on February 4, *Wisconsin* was attached to the Asiatic Fleet until it joined the battleships of the Atlantic Fleet in setting out on the trans-Pacific leg of the Great White Fleet's circumnavigation of the globe. *Wisconsin* called at ports in New Zealand, Australia, the Philippines, Japan, China, Ceylon and Egypt before transiting the Suez Canal to visit Malta, Algiers and Gibraltar on its way to Hampton Roads, where it arrived on February 22, 1909, with the rest of the fleet. The *Wisconsin* arrived in and departed from Hampton Roads many times in the years to follow, including during World War I, when it was assigned to the Coast Battleship Patrol Squadron, and later as a training ship. *Wisconsin* was permanently decommissioned on May 15, 1920, and sold for scrap less than two years later. *Courtesy of the author.*

When the USS *Wisconsin* (BB-9) made port at Albany, Western Australia, its crew was gifted Murphy, a kangaroo that quickly endeared himself to everyone aboard. As the *Wisconsin*'s mascot, Murphy learned to box, wrestle and do quite a bit of fancy skipping and jumping. But he also had a few missteps along the way. He was on the sick list for five days during the ship's transit from New Orleans to New York in April 1910 after he miscalculated an unusually long jump and fell through a hatch into the junior officers' wardroom. When the ship was put in reserve later that month, three hundred of its crew were shifted to the newly commissioned USS *Delaware* (BB-28), and Murphy went with them. *Courtesy of the author.*

The coal collier USS *Jupiter* (AC-3) was a 19,360-ton ship built at the Mare Island Navy Yard, California. *Jupiter* was commissioned in April 1913 and was the navy's first surface ship propelled by electric motors and also an engineering prototype for the turbo-electric propulsion system widely used in navy capital ships built during the later 1910s and the 1920s. *Jupiter* provided transportation and coal-carrying services for the United States Pacific Fleet until October 1914, when it transited the Panama Canal to begin operations in the Atlantic. During World War I, it carried cargo to Europe and supplied coal to combat and logistics forces on both sides of the Atlantic. *Jupiter* was decommissioned in March 1920 to begin its conversion to an aircraft carrier. Renamed *Langley* in April 1920 and designated CV-1 when the navy implemented its hull number system in July 1920, it was recommissioned two years later as the sea service's first flattop. *Jupiter* fielded a competitive baseball team, shown here, in 1913. *Courtesy of the author.*

This sailors' parade took place in downtown Norfolk on February 27, 1909, just a few days after the American fleet returned from its trip around the world. *Courtesy of the author.*

The fleet came back from around the world to new technology, including improvements to submarines. *Narwhal*, shown in this 1909 photograph, was commissioned that fall and joined the Atlantic Torpedo Fleet based at Newport, Rhode Island, shortly thereafter. This pioneer submarine was very active in the Chesapeake Bay and off Norfolk, Virginia; on target ranges proving torpedoes; on experimental operations; and in cruises up and down the East Coast. *Narwhal* was renamed *D-1*, the lead ship of its class, on November 17, 1911. *Courtesy of the George Grantham Bain Collection, Library of Congress Prints and Photographs Division.*

Two *C*-class submarines, the USS *Snapper* (*C-5*) (left) and USS *Stingray* (*C-2*) (right), were photographed pier side about 1910. The *Stingray* was commissioned on November 23, 1909, and assigned to the Atlantic Torpedo Fleet and, later, the Atlantic Submarine Flotilla, cruising up and down the East Coast until May 20, 1913, when it departed Norfolk, Virginia, for a six-month deployment operating from Guantanamo Bay, Cuba. *Snapper* was commissioned on February 2, 1910, with Lieutenant (later Fleet Admiral) Chester W. Nimitz in command. It, like *Stingray*, was assigned to the submarine flotilla and remained active along the East Coast and in the Chesapeake Bay until it departed Norfolk for Cuba. *Courtesy of the George Grantham Bain Collection, Library of Congress Prints and Photographs Division.*

The collier USS *Proteus* (AC-9) was launched (shown here) at Newport News Shipbuilding and Dry Dock Company on September 14, 1912. With the threat of war with Mexico looming, it was commissioned July 9, 1913, with Master Robert J. Easton, of the Naval Auxiliary Service, in command. This Hampton Roads–based collier coaled battleships and cruisers of the Atlantic Fleet off Mexico. *Proteus* was later assigned to the Naval Overseas Transportation Service to supply coal, oil, men and stores for ships of the Atlantic Fleet. The collier deployed in and out of Norfolk throughout its history, including service to the fleet at home and abroad during World War I. *Proteus* was lost at sea, cause unknown, sometime after November 23, 1941. Two of *Proteus*'s sister ships, USSs *Cyclops* (AC-4) and *Nereus* (AC-10), also disappeared without a trace while performing similar duties during World War I and World War II, respectively. *Courtesy of the George Grantham Bain Collection, Library of Congress Prints and Photographs Division.*

The crew of a United States Navy coaling ship was photographed at Hampton Roads in February, circa 1915. *Courtesy of the author.*

Crewman William R. Heiss, a musician first class, took this picture of the *Connecticut*-class battleship USS *Minnesota* (BB-22) being coaled in June 1910. Sailors aboard *Minnesota* are moving coal carts across its deck. *Minnesota* was laid down at Newport News Shipbuilding on October 27, 1903, launched on April 8, 1905, and commissioned on March 9, 1907, and, after fitting out, was assigned duty in connection with the Jamestown Exposition from April 22 to September 3, 1907. President Theodore Roosevelt then sent *Minnesota* around the world with the Great White Fleet. After the fleet's return to Hampton Roads on February 22, 1909, *Minnesota* was assigned to the Atlantic Fleet; it was decommissioned on December 1, 1921. *Courtesy of the author.*

The battleship USS *Wyoming* (BB-32) was the lead ship of its class. Commissioned on September 25, 1912, it reached Hampton Roads on December 30 to become the flagship of Rear Admiral Charles Johnston Badger, commander, United States Atlantic Fleet. *Wyoming* spent much of its service life in the Chesapeake Bay, specifically Hampton Roads. This photograph shows United States Marines aboard *Wyoming* in May 1913. *Courtesy of the Library of Congress Prints and Photographs Division.*

Interned German sailors constructed this miniature German village at the Norfolk Navy Yard just prior to America's entry into World War I. It was during 1915 that two German raiders, *Prinz Eitel Friedrich* and *Kronprinz Wilhelm*, were chased into Hampton Roads by British warships. The United States impounded both raiders, shown here, and their crews were quartered at the navy yard. The village included streets, houses, public buildings and a church. After the United States entered the war on April 6, 1917, the Germans became prisoners of war and were removed from the Norfolk Navy Yard. *Courtesy of the author.*

Chapter 5

Wings of Gold

The Norfolk Navy Yard played host to one of the world's most momentous events—the first flight of an airplane off a United States Navy warship—in November 1910. Eugene Burton Ely's aircraft, the Curtiss *Hudson Flyer*, was transported to the navy yard from Pine Beach by the naval tug *Nice*. On the evening of November 13, the *Hudson Flyer*'s engine, due to be delivered by boat from Baltimore, hadn't arrived, so Ely boarded a ferry to Portsmouth to find his mechanics. After the *Hudson Flyer* was craned aboard the ship, it was secured aft on the platform, its tail tied just over the scout cruiser USS *Birmingham*'s (CL-2) ship's wheel. This left only fifty-seven feet of platform for takeoff.

After *Birmingham* left its berth at the navy yard the morning of November 14, it steamed down the Elizabeth River between Norfolk and Portsmouth headed for Hampton Roads, accompanied by two destroyers, one of which stopped in Norfolk to fetch Ely's wife, Mabel, and the growing pool of newspaper reporters who now knew this was a story they didn't want to miss. Ely helped his mechanics install the plane's engine, a task they completed by the time the *Birmingham* had passed Pine Beach and headed into the harbor. By then it was joined by four torpedo craft, the USSs *Bailey*, *Rowe*, *Stringham* and *Terry*. *Rowe*, the fastest craft on station, was positioned closest to the *Birmingham* in case Ely was unsuccessful on takeoff or mid-flight; its crew might need to pluck Ely from the stormy water of the Roads. The *Rowe* was also the press boat. Ely's original destination on takeoff from the *Birmingham* was the marine barracks parade ground at the navy yard. But he didn't make it that far. He landed at Willoughby Beach in the vicinity of Ocean View. Deteriorating weather conditions were to blame. Had the weather been better, he intended to fly beyond the Rip Raps, rounding Sewell's Point, Lambert's Point and following the center of the Elizabeth River over the inner harbor, turning to the south and then above the county ferry wharf and going directly to the navy yard. His original flight would have taken forty minutes. The actual one took only four minutes. But Ely's flight was just the beginning, and to most purists it was and will remain the start of United States naval aviation. Two months later, on January 18, 1911, Ely landed his Curtiss pusher aboard the armored cruiser USS *Pennsylvania* (ACR-4), anchored in San Francisco Bay.

Ely's successful flights were soon followed by others, though not all would end up front-page news. Ely wouldn't live long enough to know the names of the men who'd come after him. He was killed at the end of an October 19, 1911 exhibition flight in Macon, Georgia. Six days later, Navy Lieutenants Theodore Gordon "Spuds" Ellyson, Naval Aviator No. 1, and John Henry "Jack" Towers, Naval Aviator No. 3, set out in a Curtiss A-1 Triad from Greenbury Point, Annapolis, Maryland, to Buckroe Beach, in proximity to Newport News, Virginia. The successful A-1 Triad flight marked the beginning of a succession of firsts of flight for naval aviation. Ellyson and Towers were followed into the history books by Lieutenant Patrick Neison Lynch "Pat" Bellinger, Naval Aviator No. 8, who flew a tailless Burgess-Dunne AH-10 to Hampton Roads to spot army mortar fire from Fort Monroe's shore batteries from the air between August 5–6, 1915. This was the first time that ground fire was observed from an aircraft. From that point forward, naval aviation's rapid advances at Hampton Roads often and easily eclipsed early records. The earliest records to fall were those set by Ellyson and Towers on their 1911 flight from Greenbury Point to Buckroe Beach.

What eventually became Naval Air Station Norfolk, now Naval Station Norfolk Chambers Field, had its roots firmly planted at Naval Air Detachment, Curtiss Field, Newport News, Virginia, where naval aviators were trained before the navy got an air station up and running at its newly christened operating base on the Norfolk side of Hampton Roads. Aviation pioneer Glenn Curtiss established his flying school and experimental station at Newport News in 1915, and it was there that America's first naval aviators were trained before the Navy Department moved its flight training facility to the northeastern corner of 143 acres of land on which it started building its new naval station. Though established May 19, 1917, it would be nearly five months before the five officers, three aviators, ten enlisted sailors and seven aircraft were renamed Naval Air Detachment, Naval Operating Base, Hampton Roads. The detachment's seaplanes were flown across the James River and moored to stakes in the water off the naval station until canvas hangars were built. The new location offered sheltered water in an ice-free harbor, ideal for seaplane operations, good anchorage on the beachfront, accessibility to supplies and the operating base and room for expansion.

When America's first naval aviators arrived at the few acres that had been set aside for their use, it was a blank canvas. Large white hangars, temporary wooden buildings, were hastily thrown up, some partly concealed by huge canvas tents full of airplanes. But all of this, despite its temporary nature, was an improvement over seaplanes moored in open water and vulnerable to weather, saltwater damage and deterioration. The navy planned to build permanent concrete and steel hangars, but with America's involvement in World War I it was more important to train pilots. By the fall of 1917, it was clear to the Navy Department that Hampton Roads' climate and East Coast location would make the naval air installation there one of the most important bases of its kind in the country. By June 1918, with the exception of Naval Air Station Pensacola, Florida, Norfolk had become the most significant flying station in the navy for flight experimentation, patrol operations and advance training of naval aviators.

The navy's experimental and test department, collocated with the Hampton Roads air detachment on January 1, 1918, made so many strides forward for naval aviation that only brief mention can be made of them here. Years would pass before anyone outside those involved would recognize the extent to which major inventors were brought to the Hampton Roads air station to conduct sophisticated research and experimentation in aviation communication, largely radio telegraphy and radio telephony, that enabled airborne pilots to communicate with men on the ground. Bellinger recalled in later years, "Many celebrated radio engineers and inventors found their way to us, especially Lee de Forest. One day the radio officer came to me and said, 'If you come with me, you can talk to and hear the pilot of a plane in the air.' I went with him, tried the phone and talked to the plane in the air. It seems strange to say so now, but it was then a weird sensation to be talking to a man flying in a plane. The test worked perfectly, and I believe it was the first really successful test of the kind."

Bellinger, the air station's first commanding officer, witnessed great advances not only with test and evaluation of aircraft but also with his active lighter-than-air operation. The navy's Dirigible and Balloon School was located at Hampton Roads until 1924, when it was moved to Naval Air Station Lakehurst, New Jersey. Norfolk's main airship hangar was disassembled and relocated to Lakehurst, but during World Wars I and II airships, later blimps, were used for antisubmarine patrol. Airship operations, even experimentation, continued at Hampton Roads and bases under its operational control, despite the school's move to Lakehurst, for as long as the navy continued its lighter-than-air program. But there was more, much more, from aircraft world's records and technological and hardware advances to periods of war and peace that added quickly to the air station's bona fides. Bellinger saw temporary canvas hangars give way to wood frame barracks, a mess hall, an administration building, a dispensary, aircraft shops and hangars. Then, on August 27, 1918, what had begun as a small naval air detachment was designated Naval Air Station Hampton Roads, a status that made it a separate command from the adjacent naval operating base. In August 1932, the air station's name was officially changed to Naval Air Station Norfolk, and on June 1, 1938, its first airfield was named Chambers Field in honor of Captain Washington Irving Chambers, the first officer in charge of naval aviation and director of the navy's early efforts to find a home for aircraft in the fleet. In its first quarter century, Naval Air Station Norfolk had become synonymous with the birth of naval aviation.

Captain Washington Irving Chambers was in charge of aviation correspondence in the office of the secretary of the navy, and it was while in this capacity that he became keenly interested in the possibilities of bringing aircraft into the fleet. Convinced an aircraft could be launched from a ship, he approved the use of the scout cruiser USS *Birmingham* (CL-2), from which Curtiss Exhibition Company pilot Eugene Burton Ely made his November 14, 1910 flight at Hampton Roads. Chambers Field at Naval Station Norfolk was named in his honor. *Official United States Navy Photograph.*

Ely's Curtiss *Hudson Flyer* was hoisted aboard the *Birmingham* on the morning of November 14, 1910, at Norfolk Navy Yard, Portsmouth, Virginia. *Courtesy of the Hampton Roads Naval Museum.*

The moment when Eugene Ely's *Hudson Flyer* lifted from the deck of the *Birmingham* was captured by a photographer aboard an escort ship. Seconds after the picture was taken, Ely dipped below *Birmingham*'s deck and skimmed along the water's surface before gaining altitude. Ely's successful flight was the first by a fixed-wing aircraft from the deck of a United States Navy ship. *Courtesy of the Hampton Roads Naval Museum.*

Eugene Ely added another first two months later, when, on January 18, 1911, he landed his Curtiss pusher aboard the armored cruiser USS *Pennsylvania* (ACR-4), anchored in San Francisco Bay. His landing was aided by the first arresting gear, a tailhook designed and built by aviator Hugh Armstrong Robinson. Ely's storied career came to a tragic end when he was killed at an aviation meet in Macon, Georgia, on October 19, 1911. This photograph shows the *Pennsylvania*'s flight deck with Ely's pusher loaded aboard. *Courtesy of the George Grantham Bain Collection, Library of Congress Prints and Photographs Division.*

Had Eugene Ely not died at Macon, Georgia, in October 1911, "[Charles] Lindbergh would have had to look for his laurels," observed Captain Norman Gillette, commanding officer of Naval Air Station Norfolk, in 1961. "Ely was far ahead of Lindbergh and might have made the Atlantic flight far earlier." Ely's flying career lasted only eighteen months. But in that brief time, he was the first man to fly from and to a naval vessel, and thus the man who first proved that naval aviation was possible. The modern aircraft carrier became the logical culmination of Ely's flights in 1910 and 1911. *Courtesy of the George Grantham Bain Collection, Library of Congress Prints and Photographs Division.*

Naval Aviator No. 1, Theodore Gordon "Spuds" Ellyson, was a Richmond, Virginia native and United States Naval Academy graduate, class of 1901, whose naval career began with battleships and submarines. He served aboard USSs *Texas, Missouri, Pennsylvania, Colorado* and *West Virginia*, among others, and was present at Newport News Shipbuilding when the submarine USS *Seal* was fitted out. He was *Seal*'s commanding officer just after its December 10, 1910 commissioning. But then Ellyson was ordered to San Diego for flight instruction under Glenn Curtiss. Later in Ellyson's storied career, on January 10, 1921, he was ordered to Hampton Roads for eight months as executive officer of the naval air station and, after that, headed back to Washington, D.C., to head the plans division at the newly minted Bureau of Aeronautics. But on June 23, 1926, he returned to Norfolk, ordered to duty on the aircraft carrier USS *Lexington* (CV-2) for its fitting out and commissioning. Commander Ellyson was killed on February 27, 1928, his forty-third birthday, when his aircraft crashed in the lower Chesapeake Bay on a night flight from Norfolk to Annapolis. He is shown here in 1911. *Courtesy of the Library of Congress Prints and Photographs Division.*

The *Tennessee*-class armored cruiser USS *North Carolina* (ACR-12) was the first ship equipped with an aircraft catapult, and in 1915 it carried Curtiss N-9 seaplanes. *North Carolina* was laid down at Newport News Shipbuilding on March 21, 1905, and commissioned at Norfolk Navy Yard on May 7, 1908. Several years later, on September 9, 1915, *North Carolina* made a major contribution to the advancement of naval aviation while serving as Naval Air Station Pensacola's station ship. On November 5, 1915, it became the first ship to launch an aircraft, a Curtiss Model F, by catapult while underway. This experiment led to the use of catapults on battleships and cruisers through World War II and, importantly, to the development of steam catapults on modern-day aircraft carriers. *Official United States Navy Photograph.*

The Gallaudet Aircraft Corporation reorganized and moved to new headquarters facilities at Greenwich, Rhode Island, in the spring of 1917. The company produced two D-4 aircraft for the United States Navy: Bureau Nos. A2653 and A2654. The latter aircraft was photographed at Hampton Roads. The D-4 was powered by a Liberty engine and could reach about ninety miles per hour at top speed. *Official United States Navy Photograph.*

Two Curtiss H-12 flying boats, Bureau Nos. A781 and A770, were photographed in 1917 at what would soon become Naval Air Station Hampton Roads. The H-12 was the new, improved version of the flying boat ordered by Rodman Wanamaker in 1914, called the *America,* which he planned to fly over the Atlantic. When the United States Navy ordered an upgraded version in 1916, it was designated the H-12, though airmen called it "Large America," recalling Wanamaker's aircraft. Only nineteen H-12s were built, including the two shown here. *Courtesy of the Hampton Roads Naval Museum.*

This Boeing Aeromarine seaplane belonged to Naval Air Detachment Hampton Roads and was photographed February 14, 1918, in front of what airmen called "Tent City." The tents were used for everything from sailors' living quarters to aircraft storage and repair. *Official United States Navy Photograph.*

A hydrogen-filled airship landed across the high-tension wires of a hangar near Naval Air Station Hampton Roads's administrative building on July 24, 1918, and set it and several other buildings on fire. Most of the new air station burned that day. *Official United States Navy Photograph.*

This was all that remained of barracks on the air station after they caught fire in July 1918. The skeletal remains of the airship that struck high-tension wires came to rest in the smoldering debris (center). *Courtesy of the author.*

An experimental triplane, possibly the Curtiss L-type, was photographed at Naval Air Station Hampton Roads on July 15, 1918. Two holdovers from the 1907 Jamestown Exposition loom large behind the aircraft: the Grand Basin and its prominent stone bridge, gifted to the exposition by the Japanese government. The buildings left and right, stretching down the piers and shore, belonged to the air station. *Courtesy of the Hampton Roads Naval Museum.*

Naval Air Station Hampton Roads administrative heads were photographed in late 1918. *Seated in the front row, second from left*, was Lieutenant Ganson Goodyear "Gans" Depew, United States Naval Reserve (USNR), Naval Aviator No. 121, who served as flight superintendent and executive officer; and, *third from left*, Lieutenant Commander Patrick Neison Lynch Bellinger, Naval Aviator No. 8, commanding officer. *Back row, standing fourth from left*, was Lieutenant (junior grade) Robert Livingston "Liv" Ireland, USNR, Naval Aviator No. 84; *fifth from left*, Lieutenant John Vorys, Naval Aviator No. 73; and, *sixth from left*, Lieutenant Louis Theodore Barin, Naval Aviator No. 56, a well-known experimental test pilot who was killed in an accident at Rockwell Field, North Island, San Diego, California, on June 12, 1920. Ireland was detailed as officer in charge of Naval Air Station Morehead City, North Carolina, in September 1918, a patrol station under Bellinger's command. *Courtesy of the Hampton Roads Naval Museum.*

Sailors attached to the fledgling naval aviation detachment at Hampton Roads were photographed in early summer 1918 moving a Curtiss R-9 aircraft into the waters of the Grand Basin area, a holdover from the 1907 Jamestown Exposition. Rising above the tents is the tower of Pennsylvania House, a replica of Philadelphia's Independence Hall also built for the exposition. *Courtesy of the Hampton Roads Naval Museum.*

A Curtiss H-12 flying boat, Bureau No. A769, photographed on May 29, 1918, at Hampton Roads, had extensive damage to its upper wing and equally troubling engine problems. Naval aviators, maintenance officers and enlisted ground crew were assessing the aircraft's damage to make repairs when this picture was taken. *Courtesy of the Hampton Roads Naval Museum.*

The pilot of a kite balloon climbed a rope ladder to get aboard. This picture was taken at Naval Training Center Hampton Roads on May 29, 1918, and is one of several sequential photographs of this kite balloon from preflight preparation to full flight inscribed with this date. *Courtesy of the Library of Congress Prints and Photographs Division.*

A Curtiss H-16 flying boat sunk at Hampton Roads on July 30, 1918. Sailors on boats to the left and right of the aircraft tied on lines to keep it above water, but it was a battle they were not going to win. Seawater poured through the H-16's crew compartments and swamped its interior. The weight of the water soon carried it under. *Courtesy of the Hampton Roads Naval Museum.*

To check the depth of the water and the draft of the R-9 aircraft pictured here, a sailor took draft readings while the aircraft was at full-load capacity, thus the need to have an aircrew seated in the cockpit. This photograph was taken August 8, 1918, at Naval Air Station Hampton Roads, and the participants were attached to its naval air detachment. *Courtesy of the Hampton Roads Naval Museum.*

A naval aviator released Peerless Pilot circa 1918. This remarkable pigeon delivered over 150 messages during World War I. The last seventy-five pigeons in the United States Navy were auctioned at Naval Air Station Hampton Roads in December 1929; all sold for the meager sum of sixty dollars to a Norfolk man. *Official United States Navy Photograph.*

Three C-class airships were assigned to Naval Air Station Hampton Roads, including the
C-3, Bureau No. A4120, shown here; C-7, Bureau No. 4127; and C-9, Bureau No. 4124.
C-3 was manufactured by Goodyear and delivered to Hampton Roads in February 1919,
when this picture was taken. C-3 was destroyed by fire when a spark from its engine ignited
it near the air station on July 8, 1921. *Official United States Navy Photograph.*

Built at Newport News Shipbuilding and commissioned October 13, 1919, the fleet oiler USS *Patoka* (AO-9) was chosen in 1924 as a tender for the navy's rigid airships USSs *Shenandoah* (ZR-1), *Los Angeles* (ZR-3) and *Akron* (ZR-4). *Patoka* was fitted with a mooring mast that rose about 125 feet above the water; space to accommodate the airship's crews and equipment; facilities for the helium, gasoline and other supplies necessary for *Shenandoah* to operate; and handling and stowage facilities for three seaplanes. This work was completed at the Norfolk Navy Yard shortly after July 1, 1924. *Patoka* conducted the first successful mooring experiments with *Shenandoah*, shown here, on August 8, 1924. *Courtesy of the George Grantham Bain Collection, Library of Congress Prints and Photographs Division.*

The Navy/Curtiss NC-9 flying boat, Bureau No. A5885, was built by the Naval Aircraft Factory (NAF) and delivered to Norfolk in the spring of 1921, permanently assigned to the Atlantic Fleet Air Detachment. This aircraft's linen-covered upper wing measured 126 feet from wingtip to wingtip, and the lower wing was 94 feet across; the fuselage was a little over 86 feet long. The NAF initially built just four of these flying boats, including the NC-4, which successfully crossed the Atlantic in May 1919. But NC-5–NC-10 soon followed. NC-9 was stricken from the navy inventory on May 20, 1924, after flight engineers determined it was no longer sea or flight worthy. *Courtesy of the author.*

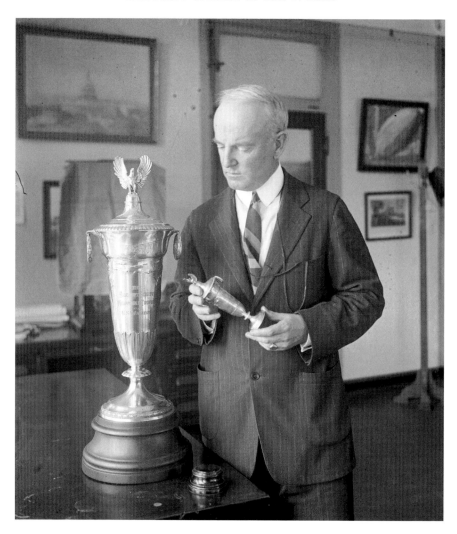

Rear Admiral William Adger Moffett, shown here on June 10, 1925, with the Herbert Schiff Memorial Trophy, was the first chief of the Bureau of Aeronautics and one of the great figures of American aviation. He also made frequent appearances at Hampton Roads. Appointed chief on September 1, 1921, Moffett's tenure was marked with great strides forward for naval aviation, including the development of the first successful radial engines, the Norden bombsight, metal seaplane hulls and a series of racing aircraft that in 1923 gave the United States Navy twenty-three world records. He was designated naval observer no. 1. Moffett lost his life on April 4, 1933, during a test flight aboard the dirigible USS *Akron*, which crashed off Barnegat Light, New Jersey. The Schiff trophy was named for Lieutenant (junior grade) Herbert Schiff, who was killed in an accident at Naval Air Station Hampton Roads on July 11, 1924. From 1925 to 1928, the trophy was awarded to the naval aviator who compiled the highest number of flying hours in one year without serious accident or injury involving personnel or aircraft. The first competitive year was July 1, 1924, to June 30, 1925. The 1925 winner was Lieutenant (junior grade) Reginald de Noyes Thomas, Naval Aviator No. 207. From 1929, the trophy went to a squadron. *Courtesy of the Library of Congress Prints and Photographs Division.*

Chapter 6
Big Guns

The United States' entry into World War I on April 6, 1917, was precipitated by Germany's extension of unrestricted submarine warfare to America's East Coast. With the nation at war and merchant ships in the cross hairs of German U-boats, the sea service had little trouble filling vacancies in the fleet. Just before President Woodrow Wilson's declaration of war against Germany, the administration sent Rear Admiral William Sowden Sims to London as its naval representative. Sims, then serving as president of the Naval War College, had long impressed his superiors in Washington as an unwavering advocate of fleet modernization. After the United States' entry into the war, Sims was sent back to London. But this time he was given command over American naval forces operating from Great Britain. His role was significant. Sims quickly assessed that the British didn't have the fleet to win the U-boat war. They needed help. He appealed to the Navy Department to send all its available destroyers, cruisers, submarines and auxiliaries to supplant the British fleet. The navy immediately dispatched six destroyers—the USSs *Davis* (DD-65), *Conyngham* (DD-58), *McDougal* (DD-54), *Porter* (DD-59), *Wadsworth* (DD-60) and *Wainwright* (DD-62)—under the command of an officer familiar to Hampton Roads, Commander Joseph Knefler Taussig. After making a quick transit across the storm- and gale-filled Atlantic, Taussig was asked by Commander in Chief of the Coasts of Ireland Admiral Lewis Bayly when he would be ready to go on patrol. Taussig replied in his now famous words, "We are ready now, Sir," adding, "that is, as soon as we can finish fueling."

What Great Britain needed just as much as Taussig's destroyers were "the big guns." What they got was Rear Admiral Hugh Rodman's Battleship Division Nine, its escorts and auxiliaries, which left Hampton Roads on November 25, 1917, bound for Scapa Flow to strengthen the British Grand Fleet. Battleship Division Nine arrived on December 7, 1917, joining British naval forces in blockade and escort missions. Rodman's division became one of the most successful deterrents to major German naval action for the rest of the war. But it had been Sims's initiative that put them there. Sims ended the war as a vice admiral in command of all United States naval forces operating in Europe. And he earned it. Sims cajoled the British Royal Navy to employ the convoy system to build back its overseas supply lines. He got them to use Taussig's and their own destroyers to escort merchant ships through waters crawling with German U-boats. Hampton Roads played a critical role, transporting goods through its ports to support the war effort. A large part of what became the Naval Overseas Transportation Service, established in 1918, operated from Norfolk.

Hampton Roads was a busy place during World War I. With America at war, an early decision was made to expand the Norfolk Navy Yard, including construction of dry docks numbers four, six and seven, none of which was finished until 1919. A number of ships interned in the United States before America joined the war were seized from Germany and sent to the yard to be converted, among them the *Pennsylvania*, *Neckar* and *Rhein*. The first was rechristened *Nansemond*; the second became the *Antigone*; and the third was the *Susquehanna*. These steamers supplemented the United States' troop transport fleet. Many new shop facilities were added at the shipyard, where 11,234 workers found employment, a far cry from the 2,718 who were there in 1914. During the war years, warships were repaired, converted and fitted out, but four destroyers were also built, including the 1,020-ton *Caldwell*-class destroyer *Craven* (DD-70), launched in 1918; and the USSs *Hulbert* (DD-342), *Noa* (DD-343) and *William B. Preston* (DD-344), launched in 1919. The 43,200-ton battleship USS *North Carolina* (BB-52) was constructed at the yard, too, and though more than a third complete, this ship, more powerful than any then in the fleet, was scrapped in 1923 as a result of the Washington Naval Limitation Treaty. While World War I increased ship construction and repair, it also limited the mission of the Norfolk Navy Yard.

The USS *Rhode Island* (BB-17) rotated in and out of Hampton Roads during its service life. Commissioned February 19, 1906, it underwent extensive shakedown and acceptance trials between Hampton Roads and Boston. *Rhode Island* arrived in Hampton Roads on December 8, 1907, to join fifteen other battleships, a torpedo boat squadron and transports for the great fleet review that culminated in the Great White Fleet's cruise around the world. Upon its return, *Rhode Island* remained in the Atlantic. During much of World War I, it was based from Hampton Roads. At war's end, it transported over five thousand American troops from Brest, France, to Hampton Roads and Boston. *Courtesy of the George Grantham Bain Collection, Library of Congress Prints and Photographs Division.*

The *Tennessee*-class armored cruiser USS *Washington* (ACR-11), later renamed *Seattle*, was commissioned on August 7, 1906, and was often spotted in Hampton Roads and Lynnhaven Bay. The cruiser arrived April 12, 1907, to participate in Jamestown Exposition festivities and remained into May; it did not make the cruise with the Great White Fleet. From December 20, 1910, to January 2, 1911, *Washington* underwent repairs at the Norfolk Navy Yard, where it returned again in the years to come. This stereoscopic view dates to the *Washington*'s post-commissioning period and refers to it as the "race horse" of the United States Navy. *Courtesy of the author.*

The armored cruiser USS *Washington* was renamed *Seattle* on November 9, 1916. *Seattle* was decommissioned June 28, 1946, and struck from the Naval Vessel Register July 19, 1946. The engine room of the *Washington* is shown in this pre-1916 photograph. *Courtesy of the George Grantham Bain Collection, Library of Congress Prints and Photographs Division.*

The USS *Delaware* (BB-28), the lead ship of its class, was launched at Newport News Shipbuilding and Dry Dock Company on February 6, 1909, and commissioned on April 4, 1910. *Delaware* was assigned to the Atlantic Fleet, sailing from Hampton Roads through the end of World War I. Toward the end of its service life, *Delaware* participated in the April 28, 1921 Naval Review at Hampton Roads. *Delaware* entered Norfolk Navy Yard on August 30, 1923, and its crew was transferred to its replacement, the newly commissioned USS *Colorado* (BB-45); it was decommissioned on November 10, 1923, and later sold for scrap in accordance with the 1922 Washington Naval Limitation Treaty. *Courtesy of the Library of Congress Prints and Photographs Division.*

The USS *Virginia* (BB-13), lead ship of its class, was built at Newport News Shipbuilding and Dry Dock Company. Commissioned on May 7, 1906, *Virginia* would be inextricably tied to Hampton Roads, from its first shakedown cruise off Lynnhaven Bay to the ship's many assignments in and out of Norfolk and its stops for repair and alteration at the Norfolk Navy Yard. *Virginia* was one of sixteen battleships that went around the world with the Great White Fleet, and it is shown here preparing to depart for Mexico, one of several trips it would make between 1913 and 1914. *Courtesy of the Library of Congress Prints and Photographs Division.*

The USS *Pennsylvania* (BB-38) was laid down October 27, 1913, by Newport News Shipbuilding and Dry Dock Company and launched March 16, 1915. The *Pennsylvania* was sponsored by Elizabeth Kolb, who was invited to sponsor the country's and the world's largest battleship at the behest of Pennsylvania governor Martin Grove Brumbaugh. She was the daughter of Colonel Louis J. Kolb of Philadelphia. Elizabeth Kolb (center, holding the champagne bottle) arrived at the launch ceremony with her maids of honor, sister Katherine Kolb, Katherine Martin and Mildred Harold (all shown here). *Courtesy of the Library of Congress Prints and Photographs Division.*

Governor Martin Brumbaugh stood on the christening platform with Elizabeth Kolb just prior to her breaking the bottle of champagne over the battleship *Pennsylvania*'s bow on March 16, 1915. *Courtesy of the Library of Congress Prints and Photographs Division.*

The USS *Pennsylvania* (BB-38) was one of only two oil-burning American battleships when it officially joined the fleet on June 12, 1916, the day of its commissioning; the other oil burner was USS *Nevada* (BB-36). The world's largest dreadnought became the flagship of the United States Atlantic Fleet four months later. Elizabeth Kolb was photographed just as she swung the bottle of champagne that christened *Pennsylvania* and sent it down the ways. *Courtesy of the Library of Congress Prints and Photographs Division.*

As the battleship *Pennsylvania* slid down the ways at Newport News Shipbuilding on the morning of March 16, 1915, shown here, the twenty-thousand-plus onlookers who had come from Pennsylvania, Maryland and Virginia to watch the launch witnessed the birth of one of the greatest battleships in American history. At the time of the Japanese attack on Pearl Harbor, December 7, 1941, BB-38 was in the Pearl Harbor Navy Yard. The Japanese failed, despite repeated attempts, to sink *Pennsylvania* in its dry dock. Though it was otherwise peppered by bombs and bullets, the ship's crew continued to fire on attacking Japanese torpedo planes and dive bombers. *Pennsylvania* fought its way through the end of World War II, earning a record eight battle stars. The ship was decommissioned August 29, 1946. *Courtesy of the Library of Congress Prints and Photographs Division.*

After the United States entered World War I on April 6, 1917, the USS *New York* (BB-34) (foreground), under the command of Captain Edward L. Beach, became the flagship of Battleship Division Nine, which was a division of four, later five, dreadnought battleships of the United States Atlantic Fleet commanded by Rear Admiral Hugh Rodman. *New York* is shown leading the division out of Hampton Roads on November 25, 1917, bound for Scapa Flow to strengthen the British Grand Fleet. Battleship Division Nine arrived on December 7, 1917, joining British naval forces in blockade and escort missions. *New York* and its sister battleships' display of "big guns" deterred the Germans from launching any major naval engagements for the duration of the war. *Courtesy of the Library of Congress Prints and Photographs Division.*

The original ships of Battleship Division Nine under Rear Admiral Hugh Rodman's command included USSs *New York* (BB-34), *Delaware* (BB-28), *Florida* (BB-30) and *Wyoming* (BB-32). *Delaware*, the oldest ship in the division, was later replaced by USS *Arkansas* (BB-34) and sent home. Rodman specifically requested that *New York*'s sister ship, the powerful USS *Texas* (BB-35), be dispatched to Scapa Flow. Rodman was photographed by George Grantham Bain circa 1917. *Courtesy of the Library of Congress Prints and Photographs Division.*

United States Navy battleships sailed with elaborate silver services gifted to them by their namesake states. USS *Mississippi* (BB-23) operated frequently from Norfolk, Virginia, after its February 1, 1908 commissioning at the Philadelphia Navy Yard. *Mississippi* made its debut at Hampton Roads during the February 22, 1909 return of the Great White Fleet. But it was a short first visit. *Mississippi* soon sailed for the Caribbean, from which it departed on May 1 to cruise up the Mississippi River, calling at its major ports. *Mississippi* arrived at Natchez on May 20 and, five days later, Horn Island, where it was gifted a silver service from the State of Mississippi, a piece of which is shown here. *Courtesy of the George Grantham Bain Collection, Library of Congress Prints and Photographs Division.*

Sailors had come ashore at Old Point Comfort, Virginia, for a gun drill when this picture was taken. The original Chamberlin Hotel is to the left. The photograph was made into a real picture postcard that was mailed from Hampton, Virginia, on December 5, 1914. *Courtesy of the author.*

The USS *North Dakota*'s sailors were photographed loading coal on April 20, 1914; several of them are covered in coal dust, head to toe. A few days later, the *Delaware*-class battleship *North Dakota* (BB-29) was sent to Veracruz, Mexico, to protect American interests, arriving on April 26, 1914. The ship's sailors occupied the city. *North Dakota* returned to Norfolk, Virginia, on October 16 and started an intensive training program in anticipation of America's entry into World War I. *Courtesy of the George Grantham Bain Collection, Library of Congress Prints and Photographs Division.*

Throughout World War I, *North Dakota* operated in the York River, Virginia, and also out of New York training gunners and engineers. *North Dakota* was later decommissioned at Norfolk on November 22, 1923, along with a number of other battleships, under the terms of the Washington Naval Limitation Treaty. The "ND" is shown here during a stop at the New York Naval Shipyard. *Courtesy of the George Grantham Bain Collection, Library of Congress Prints and Photographs Division.*

Chapter 7

A New Home for the Fleet

As early as 1912 there was a movement underway by Norfolk community leaders to entice the United States government to take over the entire 474-acre site and remaining buildings of the 1907 Jamestown Exposition for a naval base. Five years of cajoling hadn't piqued the navy's interest, not just then. But World War I changed everything. A June 15, 1917 Act of Congress gave the president of the United States the power to take possession of the exposition property and the secretary of the navy the authority to develop Sewell's Point as a naval operating base, to include piers, storehouses, fuel oil storage, a training station and recreation grounds for the fleet, and for other purposes. President Woodrow Wilson's June 28, 1917 proclamation made it official and gave the base a name: Naval Operating Base Hampton Roads. A 1917 map that accompanied the proclamation showed that a few of the original exposition buildings still standing were the auditorium and education building, which became home to the now defunct Fifth Naval District; the history building to the west, converted to the base gymnasium; and some of the state and smaller exhibit buildings on the waterfront. The Pine Beach Hotel still stood, too. Naval officers assigned to the new operating base first made it their officers' club, but it was later also a marine barracks, among other uses, before it was razed.

Rear Admiral Walter McLean, commandant of the navy yard and Fifth Naval District commander, took over the Sewell's Point property for the navy on July 4, 1917. But he delegated construction of the new base to Rear Admiral Albert Caldwell Dillingham. This original acreage is now a small part of present Naval Station Norfolk. Due to construction delays, the new base wouldn't be commissioned until October 12, a day celebrated by the transfer of 1,400 sailors from Saint Helena Naval Training Center in Norfolk's Berkley section. All 1,400 of them, accompanied by two artillery battalions, an eighteen-piece band and a bugle corps, marched through Norfolk to their new base. Rear Admiral Dillingham delivered the commissioning speech that is best remembered for one line: "The base has begun to function." And it had.

Within its first year of operation, fleet support and shore training functions were transferred from the Norfolk Navy Yard to the new operating base, which by then quartered the Fifth Naval District; Naval Training Center Hampton Roads; Naval Air Detachment Hampton Roads, which became a naval air station on August 27, 1918; a naval hospital; and one of the navy's most important submarine stations. A map made in April 1918 indicated new barracks, mess halls, hospital, brigs, warehouses, shops, schools and hangars, and a small area designated "Aero Group," from which the storied Naval Air Station Norfolk soon sprung. There was only one pier then, Pier 2, but a plan for additional piers and submarine basin were also shown, in addition to reclamation of the water area to the north. Less than a year after, on March 1, 1919, the operating base added a naval supply station and began to provide the sea service with a central supply point on the East Coast.

When the Naval Supply Station Hampton Roads began, it had only two permanent buildings, five temporary warehouses and one wooden merchandise pier. Eight years later, in 1927, the station had grown to such an extent that it was redesignated a naval supply depot consisting of ten warehouses—five permanent and five temporary—a fuel oil station and two wooden piers. This was the beginning of today's Fleet and Industrial Supply Center (FISC). The supply center's meteoric growth between the wars was unique to the naval operating base, where overall growth slowed. The only other exception to this was naval aviation, which the General Board of the United States Navy determined in 1919 was of overriding importance to the projection of naval power in the future. The navy was otherwise hard pressed to garner political support for the surface fleet in the face of the country's postwar drawdown. The euphoria of peace blanketed the nation. The United States had fought the war to end all wars, and no one believed, not just then, that another, more horrible threat loomed large on the horizon. Soon, calls for America's neutrality replaced the trill of war, of a world turned upside down.

The USS *Franklin*, originally a screw frigate, was laid down at the Portsmouth Navy Yard in 1854 and built, in part, from materials salvaged from its predecessor, *Franklin*. *Franklin* was placed out of commission at Norfolk, Virginia, on March 2, 1877, and recommissioned the same day as a receiving ship for Naval Station Norfolk, continuing in this service until October 14, 1915, which marked its final decommissioning. The *Franklin* was stricken from the Naval Vessel Register on October 26, 1915, and sold. Before any of this happened, it was alive with a crew that fielded a championship baseball team, led to victory in 1913 by Lieutenant Commander George Loring Porter Stone, pictured left with his team. *Courtesy of the author.*

The submarine USS *L-1*, the first of its class, was photographed in Hampton Roads on December 13, 1916, eight months after it was commissioned. Designed by the Electric Boat Company, the *L-1* was used in East Coast waters until World War I broke out, when it was sent overseas. When *L-1* returned to the East Coast in 1919, it was used for experimental purposes until decommissioning in April 1922. *Courtesy of the Library of Congress Prints and Photographs Division.*

During World War I, the Norfolk Navy Yard underwent dramatic growth. Three new dry docks were begun between 1917 and 1919, none of which was finished before 1919. The yard employed 11,234 workers, a record at that time and a significant uptick from the 2,718 men and women employed there in June 1914. Portsmouth's Cradock and Truxtun communities, two wartime housing projects, were constructed to accommodate new yard workers and their families. The opening ceremony for Dry Dock Nos. 6 and 7 took place on October 31, 1919. This photograph, from that day, shows the admission of first water into the dry docks. *Courtesy of the Hampton Roads Naval Museum.*

Sailors held a burial service for a fallen comrade during World War I. *Courtesy of the author.*

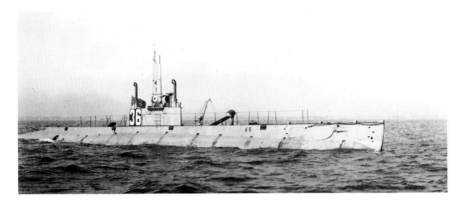

The *K-1*-class submarine *K-5* No. 36 was photographed in Hampton Roads on December 13, 1916. Commissioned in August 1914, it patrolled the East Coast and Gulf of Mexico for three years, including the first year of America's involvement in World War I. *K-5* No. 36 was decommissioned in February 1923 and laid up for a short period at Norfolk, Virginia, before being sold for scrap in June 1931. *Courtesy of the Library of Congress Prints and Photographs Division.*

The United States Navy took ownership of 474 acres of land at Sewell's Point to build Naval Operating Base Norfolk on July 4, 1917; this is now a small part of the much larger 4,631-acre naval base complex. Harry C. Mann took this picture in 1920 of the rear of the Jamestown Exposition Auditorium and Education Building, converted by the navy to house its fleet headquarters. When it was destroyed by fire on January 26, 1941, Rear Admiral Joseph K. Taussig, commandant of the Fifth Naval District, lost his headquarters, communications center, post office, district disbursing office and invaluable records critical to defense projects. The Fifth District soon got a new home—Building N-26. *Courtesy of the author.*

The Naval Operating Base Norfolk Recreation Hall interior, photographed by Harry C. Mann in 1919, was located inside the old Jamestown Exposition Education Building, a wing of the auditorium. *Courtesy of the author.*

Sailors at Naval Training Station Hampton Roads were photographed saluting the star-spangled banner on January 3, 1919. *Courtesy of the Library of Congress Prints and Photographs Division.*

Construction of a naval training camp at Hampton Roads started on July 4, 1917, and within one month enough housing for 7,500 men had been built. Within six months, the Fifth Naval District Headquarters and the naval operating base had been established. The naval operating base included the naval training center, naval air station, naval hospital and

The administration building that quartered the United States Naval Training Station Hampton Roads is shown here as it appeared on January 3, 1919. *Courtesy of the Library of Congress Prints and Photographs Division.*

a submarine station. By the end of World War I, there were 34,000 enlisted men assigned to the base. Hampton Roads's training battalion was photographed in December 1917. *Courtesy of the Library of Congress Prints and Photographs Division.*

This view of the Portsmouth Naval Hospital grounds to the east from the roof of the central powerhouse also shows the adjacent medical storage building and World War I tent camp. The picture, originally provided by the Portsmouth Naval Shipyard Museum, is dated September 26, 1918. *Courtesy of the Library of Congress Historic American Buildings Survey/ Historical American Engineering Record.*

A "sham battle" was staged at United States Naval Training Station Hampton Roads in 1918 as part of the base's practical schooling of sailors bound for the fleet. *Courtesy of the author.*

Enlisted men assigned to the naval training station at Hampton Roads were billeted in a number of different types of quarters, including these bungalows. An unknown photographer took this picture of Unit B on January 3, 1919. *Courtesy of the Library of Congress Prints and Photographs Division.*

The condition of the ground outside the air station's bulkheads was photographed on October 29, 1919. This perspective shows the airship hangar (far left), a structure that loomed large over the old Jamestown Exposition statehouses, newly constructed barracks and administration buildings. *Official United States Navy Photograph.*

This aerial view of Naval Air Station Hampton Roads, later renamed Naval Air Station Norfolk, was taken about 1923. A portion of the naval base is also shown. Development of the naval base and airfield complex in 1918 and 1919 by the United States Navy was well underway. Buildings that once entertained thousands of visitors to the 1907 Jamestown Exposition were converted to house offices and billet officers. New administration buildings, supply stores, barracks, hangars and infrastructure were also added quickly. *Courtesy of the author.*

Norfolk sailors established the Hampton Roads Glee Choir, photographed during a Washington, D.C. performance some time between 1918 and 1920. *Courtesy of the Library of Congress Prints and Photographs Division.*

Sailors taking part in a boat drill at Saint Helena's were photographed, circa 1915. *Courtesy of the George Grantham Bain Collection, Library of Congress Prints and Photographs Division.*

The United States Navy operated the Saint Helena Naval Training Station in Norfolk's Berkley section. Enlisted men and officers assigned to Saint Helena's posed for this photograph during the Fourth Liberty Loan Parade on October 11, 1918. Standing in the foreground (left to right) are Boatswain John H. Granholm, Captain Francis L. Chadwick and Lieutenant George W. Pounder. *Courtesy of the Library of Congress Prints and Photographs Division.*

Toward the end of World War I, the Salvation Army opened naval and military homes or clubs in cities where it operated and the military had a particularly high concentration of soldiers, sailors and airmen. The Salvation Army opened its Naval and Training Club at 105 West Plume Street, located in downtown Norfolk, in 1919. The name of this club was changed to the Salvation Army Naval and Military Club between 1920 and 1921, when this picture was taken of its recreation room and reproduced as a postcard. After 1921, it was known as the Salvation Army's Army Hall, later Army Hotel, and offered furnished rooms to servicemen. *Courtesy of the author.*

These young men, photographed on July 14, 1920, by George Leslie Hall, owner of G.L. Hall Optical Company of Norfolk, Virginia, were participants in the summer school held at the Naval Training Station Hampton Roads. *Courtesy of the Library of Congress Prints and Photographs Division.*

Among the men who reported to Naval Training Station Hampton Roads in the summer of 1920, these pugilists were photographed outside their tents. "This is a picture of me when I was training, taken last summer," wrote the shirtless boxer in trunks and white sneakers. *Courtesy of the author.*

Chapter 8

Between the Wars

Following the recommendation of the General Board of the United States Navy, Congress approved funding in June 1919 for the conversion of the collier USS *Jupiter* (AC-3) into the navy's first aircraft carrier, the USS *Langley* (CV-1). The work took place at the Norfolk Navy Yard from 1919 to 1922. *Langley*'s nearly three-year conversion didn't preclude naval aviators from testing flight deck arresting gear that would later be installed on *Langley* on a dummy deck at Naval Air Station Hampton Roads nor did it preclude training the carrier's future pilots. On August 11, 1921, Lieutenant Alfred Melville Pride, Naval Aviator No. 1119, conducted the first practical application of carrier arresting gear at the air station when he landed an Aeromarine onto that dummy deck and successfully caught the arresting wire. Shortly after Pride's test, the first fifteen carrier-qualified naval aviators assigned to an aircraft carrier were formed as a group in the spring of 1922, also at Naval Air Station Hampton Roads. The "firsts" achieved by naval aviators at Hampton Roads continued in rapid succession between the wars. In August 1932, the air station was renamed Naval Air Station Norfolk.

Work on the *Langley* spelled a new era for the Norfolk Navy Yard, particularly with the postwar downturn in navy shipbuilding that took place after the 1922 Washington Naval Limitation Treaty. The yard's employment figures plummeted from a wartime high of over 11,000 to 2,538, fewer than there had been in 1914. During the balance of the twenties and into the early thirties, no new ships were constructed, a condition of the treaty; thus, few improvements were made to the yard. But the freeze on shipbuilding was eventually alleviated by a battleship modernization initiative that started in

1925. Six of the fleet's oldest battleships were modernized at the Norfolk Navy Yard, including the USS *Texas* (BB-35), 1925–26; the USS *New York* (BB-34), 1926–27; the USS *Nevada* (BB-36), 1927–29; the USS *Arizona* (BB-39), 1929–31; the USS *Mississippi* (BB-41), 1931–33; and the USS *Idaho* (BB-42), 1931–34. With the passage of the National Industrial Recovery Act in July 1933, legislation which included a critically important naval construction program, the yard built and launched nine destroyers between 1934 and 1939. Between its battleship modernization program and construction of nine destroyers, yard employment spiked to 7,625 by September 1, 1939, the day, ironically, that Germany invaded Poland and the beginning of World War II in Europe.

The navy's aviation program was Congress's favorite cause célèbre with the success of *Langley* and the impressive milestones achieved by the service's naval aviators. Congress authorized additional funding to convert two 32,000-ton unfinished battle cruisers that had been canceled under the Washington Naval Limitation Treaty. They soon became the aircraft carriers USSs *Lexington* (CV-2) and *Saratoga* (CV-3). *Lexington* was commissioned on December 14, 1927, and *Saratoga* on November 16, 1927. Both were skilled conversions. But then came the revolutionary *Ranger*. On February 25, 1933, Newport News Shipbuilding and Dry Dock Company launched the 15,578-ton USS *Ranger* (CV-4), the navy's first keel-up aircraft carrier. *Ranger* was commissioned at the Norfolk Navy Yard on June 4, 1934.

Back at Sewell's Point, a familiar face returned in June 1938 to command the air station for the second time. Captain Patrick Bellinger found that what he had helped to start two decades before had become more assembly and repair plant than active airfield. Under his direction and Rear Admiral Joseph Taussig's authority as Fifth Naval District commandant, the air station was the subject of a significant land expansion and construction program begun in 1940. Taussig testified before the United States Senate Naval Affairs Committee in April 1940 that war with Japan was inevitable. He and Bellinger wanted the Norfolk air station ready for the inevitable. Improvements were nearly complete when the Japanese attacked Pearl Harbor on December 7, 1941.

The battleship USS *New York* (BB-34), the lead ship of its class, was photographed in the Norfolk Navy Yard's Dry Dock No. 4, where it underwent remodeling and modernization in the months immediately following the ship's return from the Versailles Peace Conference. *New York* participated in some of the most remarkable events of World War I at sea, including the surrender of the German High Seas Fleet in the Firth of Forth on November 21, 1918. *New York* was back on duty in the Caribbean in the spring of 1919 and soon after that joined the Pacific Fleet. *Courtesy of the author.*

A machine shop at Norfolk Navy Yard, with sailors hard at work, was photographed in 1920. *Courtesy of the author.*

Virginian-Pilot photographer Charles S. Borjes took this picture of the nation's first aircraft carrier, the USS *Langley* (CV-1), off Cape Henry, Virginia, in 1923. *Langley* was built from the bones of the USS *Jupiter* (AC-3), a coal collier decommissioned at Norfolk Navy Yard on March 24, 1920, for conversion to the nation's first flattop. The name *Langley* was chosen on April 21, and it was reclassified "CV-1." The *Jupiter*-turned-*Langley* was recommissioned on March 20, 1922, with Captain Kenneth Whiting, Naval Aviator No. 16, in command. *Courtesy of the Sargeant Memorial Room, Norfolk Public Library.*

USS *Langley*, used largely as a floating laboratory for America's early naval aviators, naval constructors and aircraft designers, was the first electrically driven ship—going back to its days as the *Jupiter*—in the fleet and held title to many naval aviation firsts. *Langley* was downgraded to a seaplane tender and its hull reclassified AV-3 in 1936; it was sunk by Japanese bombers off Tjilatjap, Java, on February 27, 1942. *Langley* is shown here at anchor off Christobal, Panama, on March 7, 1930. *Official United States Navy Photograph.*

The *Colorado*-class battleship USS *Maryland* (BB-46) was the pride of the United States Navy with its sixteen-inch guns, the first to be mounted on an American ship, and a new type of aircraft catapult. *Maryland*'s keel was laid down April 24, 1917, by Newport News Shipbuilding; it was launched on March 20, 1920. Soon after *Maryland*'s July 21, 1921 commissioning, it was dispatched to many special events of national and international importance. The "Fighting Mary" is pictured here in 1925, the year it was sent on a goodwill mission to Australia and New Zealand. *Courtesy of the author.*

Members of the USS *Maryland*'s crew are pictured in 1925 on the cruise to Australia and New Zealand. *Courtesy of the author.*

The United States Navy began experiments with aircraft and submarines in 1926. The Bureau of Aeronautics issued a contract to the Cox-Klemin Company of College Point, Long Island, New York, to build six aircraft for this purpose: Bureau Nos. A6515 to A6520. The XS-1 (A6515) was a wood and canvas twin floatplane. Aircraft designated XS-1 were fitted with a sixty-horsepower Lawrence engine, but one XS-1 was redesignated XS-2 (A6519) and fitted with a Kinner three-cylinder engine (the aircraft shown here). The submarine *S-1* was prepared to leave the pier at Norfolk for the XS-2 flight test when this picture was taken. *Courtesy of the Hampton Roads Naval Museum.*

On July 28, 1926, the *S-1*, commanded by Lieutenant Charles Bowers "Swede" Momsen, surfaced and launched the Cox-Klemin XS-2 seaplane, a submarine scout, flown by Lieutenant Dolph Chadwick "Dick" Allen, Naval Aviator No. 1639 and a respected experimental pilot. The *S-1* subsequently recovered, stored the XS-2 and submerged with the aircraft in its protective tank. Allen is shown standing on the deck of the *S-1* with the XS-2 in its storage tank. Momsen was an American pioneer in submarine rescue and invented the underwater escape device called the Momsen Lung. *Courtesy of the Hampton Roads Naval Museum.*

Airmen prepare to launch a Consolidated NY-2 biplane trainer, Bureau No. A7521, from the seaplane ramp at Naval Air Station Hampton Roads in November 1927. The United States Navy provided basic flight instruction and training in seaplane techniques, including gunnery, with the NY-2. This aircraft improved upon its NY-1 predecessor, increasing the wingspan from thirty-four to forty feet and upgrading the engine to a 220-horsepower Wright J-5 engine. *Courtesy of the National Museum of Naval Aviation.*

The aircraft carrier USS *Saratoga* (CV-3) had just left the Norfolk Navy Yard when Charles Borjes photographed it in the Elizabeth River in May 1930. Downtown Norfolk is in the background. *Courtesy of the Sargeant Memorial Room, Norfolk Public Library.*

VF-5B Striking Eagles Boeing F4B-1 aircraft populated the flight line at Naval Air Station Hampton Roads when Charles Borjes took this picture on May 7, 1930. The squadron was assigned to the USS *Lexington* (CV-2). Section leaders' aircraft are marked with a vertical band around the fuselage centered on the squadron designation letter. The cowling and top wing of the flight leaders' aircraft were also painted in the same color. *Courtesy of the Sargeant Memorial Room, Norfolk Public Library.*

The 14,500-ton USS *Ranger* (CV-4) was the first ship built as an aircraft carrier from the keel up. *Ranger's* predecessors had all been skilled conversions. The *Ranger's* keel was laid at Newport News Shipbuilding on September 26, 1931, and it was commissioned at the Norfolk Navy Yard on June 4, 1934. First Lady Lou Henry Hoover, wife of President Herbert Hoover, was *Ranger's* sponsor and Captain Arthur Leroy Bristol Jr. its first commanding officer. *Official United States Navy Photograph.*

Vought O2U-2 Corsairs assigned to Bombing Squadron Two (B) (VB-2B) Felix the Cat crowded the deck of the USS *Saratoga* (CV-3) on May 20, 1930. Felix the Cat was first adapted as a United States Navy squadron insignia in 1921 and picked up by VB-2B in 1927. Famous Felix has been in continuous use since then and is presently the squadron insignia of Strike Fight Squadron Thirty-One (VFA-31) Tomcatters, call sign "Felix," assigned to Carrier Air Wing Eight (CVW-8). *Courtesy of the Sargeant Memorial Room, Norfolk Public Library.*

VB-3B Black Panthers' Great Lakes BG-1 biplanes (left) and VB-5B Bellerophons Curtiss BF2C-1 biplanes (right) were photographed by Charles Borjes at Naval Air Station Norfolk on March 23, 1935. Both squadrons were assigned to the aircraft carrier USS *Ranger* (CV-4). The Bellerophons derived their squadron insignia from Greek mythology, specifically Bellerophon's capture of winged Pegasus and his mission to slay the three-headed Chimera by diving three times over the monster. Bellerophon took the heads of the Chimera. This myth suited VB-5B's mission: dive-bombing. The squadron's motto was "First to Attack." *Courtesy of the Sargeant Memorial Room, Norfolk Public Library.*

Lieutenant Apollo Soucek, pictured here on March 16, 1932, at the zenith of his career as the world's premier high-altitude pilot and who would attain the rank of vice admiral, was immortalized on June 4, 1957, when the airfield at Naval Air Station Oceana, the East Coast master jet base, was named in his honor. The date of the dedication ceremony fell on the same day—June 4—that Soucek set the world record for land planes when he reached 43,166 feet in an open-cockpit, single-engine aircraft in 1930. *Official United States Navy Photograph.*

Charles Borjes took this photograph of the first aircraft carrier named USS *Enterprise* (CV-6) during its January 4, 1939 arrival at Naval Station Norfolk. Newport News Shipbuilding started construction of the "Big E" on July 17, 1934, but it was not commissioned until May 12, 1938. The Big E earned twenty battle stars, the most of any American warship during World War II, before it was decommissioned on February 17, 1947. *Courtesy of the Sargeant Memorial Room, Norfolk Public Library.*

Navy–Marine Corps rivalry flared again during pregame publicity for a football game between the Marine Corps Devil Dogs and the Norfolk Navy Yard and Naval Training Station Boots. The Boots' veteran goat and beloved mascot, Uncle Billy, got a look at the competition, the Devil Dogs' bulldog, on December 1, 1937. The game was held three days later at the naval base stadium. All proceeds were donated to the Navy Relief Fund. *Courtesy of the Sargeant Memorial Room, Norfolk Public Library.*

The first airfield at Naval Air Station Norfolk to be called Chambers Field was photographed July 29, 1939. Chambers Field was named on June 1, 1938, in honor of Captain Washington Irving Chambers, the first officer in charge of aviation and director of early efforts to find a home for naval aviation in the United States Navy. *Official United States Navy Photograph.*

Harden David Vollmer photographed the *Iowa*-class battleship USS *Missouri* (BB-63) arriving at Naval Station Norfolk on May 9, 1940. By virtue of shipyard construction schedules, the "Big Mo" was the last battleship built by the United States. Commissioned on June 11, 1944, it was also the last put to sea. USS *Wisconsin* (BB-64), its *Iowa*-class sister, beat Big Mo to war. *Missouri* was the site of the September 2, 1945 Japanese surrender in Tokyo Bay, the event that marked the end of World War II. *Courtesy of the Sargeant Memorial Room, Norfolk Public Library.*

Charles Borjes took this picture on November 11, 1941, of Naval Station Norfolk sailors participating in the city's last Armistice Day parade before the outbreak of World War II. From the end of World War I, the city held its Armistice Day parade to honor those who had died in the Great War. After World War II, which required the greatest mobilization of soldiers, sailors, marines and airmen in the nation's history, and after American forces had fought in Korea, the Eighty-third Congress, at the urging of the veterans' service organizations, struck the word "Armistice" and inserted in its place the word "Veterans." With approval of this legislation, Public Law 380, on June 1, 1954, November 11 became a day to honor American veterans of all wars. *Courtesy of the Sargeant Memorial Room, Norfolk Public Library.*

Chapter 9

Remember Pearl Harbor!

Before war loomed large on the horizon, significant changes took place within the structure of the United States Navy that would last for decades to come. On November 1, 1940, the Atlantic Squadron became Patrol Force, United States Atlantic Fleet, and that December 17, Rear Admiral Ernest Joseph King was assigned its commander. This organization was short-lived. But its successor was not. On February 1, 1941, as prescribed by General Order 143, the Patrol Force was redesignated the United States Atlantic Fleet and King its commander in chief. He was also promoted to full admiral. This was more resurrection than redesignation. The title "commander in chief, Atlantic Fleet" existed between 1906 and 1923, but it was abolished, and the title "commander, Scouting Force" was first used. General Order 143 reestablished the proper title and further reorganized the American fleet into three separate fleets: Atlantic, Pacific and Asiatic. The order further stated that each fleet would be under the command of a full admiral, thus King's two-star to four-star promotion. But these weren't the only changes.

Chief of Naval Operations Admiral Harold Rainsford Stark moved to establish a two-ocean navy to confront the reality of the growing threat to the nation's security posed by the war that was already raging in Europe and Japan's saber rattling in the East. To achieve Stark's two-ocean navy, Congress stepped up shipbuilding appropriations earmarked for aircraft carriers, battleships, destroyers, cruisers, submarines and all types of auxiliary ships. The bill authorizing this initiative was signed by President Franklin Delano Roosevelt on June 14, 1940. Shipbuilding in

Hampton Roads took off, both at Norfolk Navy Yard and across the water at Newport News Shipbuilding and Dry Dock Company. A few weeks later, Roosevelt boarded the presidential yacht *Potomac* for a trip down to the Norfolk Navy Yard to confer with Rear Admiral Joseph Taussig and Rear Admiral Manley Hale Simons, the yard commander. When he arrived on July 29, the president was impressed with what he saw. From Portsmouth, he traveled by car through Norfolk to the naval operating base, where Roosevelt surveyed Taussig's expansion and improvement program in full flower, including the air station that had already earned a reputation as one of the best in the country.

Roosevelt's visit to the Norfolk Navy Yard drew attention to the nation's most important naval shipbuilding operation. Development of yard facilities surpassed its growth many times over from World War I, including its footprint in Portsmouth. From January 1, 1940, four months after the outbreak of war in Europe, to the end of the war with Japan, on September 2, 1945, a period of five years and eight months, the Norfolk Navy Yard repaired, altered, converted or otherwise worked on 6,850 naval vessels, aggregating more than 27 million tons. But the yard also built 101 new ships and landing craft for the fleet, and millions of dollars worth of manufactured products were turned out for forces afloat and other naval establishments. The yard's work during the war reached the staggering total of over $1 billion. To achieve these numbers, the yard more than doubled in size, its reservation expanding from 352.76 acres to 746.88 acres with nearly four and a quarter miles of waterfront on the Elizabeth River. A dry dock 1,100 feet in length, capable of taking the largest ship afloat, was constructed, and 685 new buildings, both permanent and temporary, were built. By February 1943, there were 42,893 workers at the yard, nearly four times the maximum employment during the prior world war. In addition to the nine destroyers built between 1934 and 1939, the yard also constructed and launched 30 major vessels during the World War II period. This number does not include 20 3,776-ton tank landing ships (LSTs) and many other smaller watercraft that came out of the yard during this time. With the end of World War II, the shipyard resumed a familiar peacetime posture, and on December 1, 1945, the Norfolk Navy Yard was renamed the Norfolk Naval Shipyard, Portsmouth, Virginia.

During World War II, the United States Navy grew its footprint in Hampton Roads. In April 1942, the navy started the Amphibious Training Base at Little Creek, located twelve miles northeast of Norfolk off what was then the Ocean View–Virginia Beach scenic highway. With the navy in a hurry to get men trained and into combat, its building program moved fast, beginning with a waterlogged bean field on one of the Whitehurst family farms. Buildings were completed at the rate of five per day. The navy's rush was understandable. The sea service's war planners foresaw landing tens of thousands of American troops on foreign beachheads under intense enemy fire. New methods and techniques of getting them there had to be developed, and the navy needed a place to do it and train men in the art of amphibious assault. But in these salad days of the war, mud and confusion combined with military urgency. The Amphibious Training Command, United States Atlantic Fleet, was officially operating as of August 1, 1943. Four bases were constructed in the Whitehurst farm area: Naval Amphibious Training Base Little Creek, United States Naval Frontier Base Little Creek and Camps Bradford and Shelton. Naval Amphibious Training Base Little Creek was set up to train crews for landing ships medium (LSM), landing craft vehicles (LCV) and other amphibious vessels. The Naval Frontier Base Little Creek was a forwarding depot for personnel and supplies in the Mediterranean and European theaters of operation. At first, Camp Bradford was a training base for navy Seabees, but in 1943 this mission was changed to train crews for the landing ships tank (LST). There was also an Armed Guard School commissioned on October 15, 1941; its purpose was the training of officers and enlisted men to man gun crews aboard merchant ships. In 1943, an Armed Guard Center was commissioned at Camp Shelton.

At the end of the war, the Amphibious Training Command trained over 200,000 naval and 160,000 army and marine personnel. The Armed Guard Center trained some 6,500 officers and 115,000 enlisted men. But this command was disestablished at war's end, replaced by the United States Naval Amphibious Base Little Creek on August 10, 1945. The former amphibious training base became Annex I, the frontier base Annex II and Camps Bradford and Shelton Annex III. At the end of 1945, these annexes covered over 1,800 acres and four thousand yards of Chesapeake Bay beachfront to accommodate amphibious training. The base's juxtaposition on the East Coast, excellent and varied beach conditions, proximity to Norfolk's naval facilities, berthing for large amphibious ships through the size of the LST and many other advantages drove the creation of the amphibious base. But the base didn't stop evolving and has grown over the years, developing into a strategic expeditionary command that has since become the fastest-growing base in Hampton Roads, known today as Joint Expeditionary Base Little Creek–Fort Story. There, too, navy, marine and army reserve personnel use its training facilities, all coordinated through the Naval and Marine Corps

Reserve Readiness Center located on the Little Creek base. Today's 2,120-acre expeditionary base is the largest of its kind in the world and is the major operating station for the United States Atlantic Fleet's amphibious forces.

In southern Virginia Beach, the navy developed the Fleet Air Defense Training Center at Dam Neck. The center was named for the 1881 lifesaving station established there on a very lonely stretch of beach where once stood two-post grain windmills called Dam Neck Mills. The over 1,100-acre center, which sits on 3.2 miles of Atlantic Ocean beachfront, was organized in 1941 as an antiaircraft school under the command of Captain Philip Daly Gallery. Gallery had no idea where he was being sent, and no one could tell him anything about his new job when his orders arrived on November 6 of that year. The orders said only "Anti-Aircraft Range, Norfolk." Some quick checking with Fifth Naval District Public Works was more informative. He found out that the navy was in the process of building two small frame buildings near a coast guard station about five miles south of Virginia Beach on the Atlantic Coast. These were the meager beginnings of the center. There, too, would be an aircraft carrier training unit and a Bureau of Ordnance test center. Like Little Creek, Dam Neck was built quickly and later enlarged after the Korean Conflict as a training center. Today called Fleet Combat Training Center Dam Neck, the base remains the navy's only open-ocean, live-firing training facility featuring major caliber weapons.

The story of Oceana, the master jet base, began on the mud flats of Princess Anne County, now Virginia Beach, nearly a decade and a half before the airfield was designated a naval air station on April 1, 1952. With the threat of war on Norfolk's doorstep, the navy had only the air station at Norfolk and two grass auxiliary fields to conduct aviation practice work. Naval Air Station Norfolk and its auxiliary practice fields were insufficient to train the large influx of carrier squadrons expected to take up residence at Norfolk. Rear Admiral Patrick Bellinger, who'd taken over as commander in chief of the Naval Air Force Atlantic, received orders from the Bureau of Aeronautics to locate four additional fields around Norfolk. "They needed more than one because they had so damn many pilots to train so fast," explained retired Captain Dexter Cleveland Rumsey II of the navy's airfield expansion. An auxiliary landing field had been in the works for Norfolk in Princess Anne County as early as 1938. The navy's choice was purposeful. The town of Oceana was sparsely populated, and land was plentiful. The navy was laying asphaltic concrete runways on December 31, 1940, and had them finished by November 1941, just days before the Japanese attacked

Pearl Harbor. Immediately after President Roosevelt declared war on Japan and Germany on December 11, navy personnel descended on the muddy airfield at Oceana, erecting nineteen Quonset huts to house 32 officers and 172 enlisted men. The first "permanent" structure to rise above the mud flats was a wooden dual-purpose building that served as the caretaker's quarters and ambulance garage.

Oceana's first administrative authority was delegated to the senior squadron commander on site. As the number of fighter squadrons increased exponentially to meet the demand for trained aircrews and new aircraft overseas, the fighter community began transitioning from Naval Air Station Norfolk's Chambers Field to the navy's outlying fields at Naval Auxiliary Air Stations Creeds, Monogram and Pungo and Naval Auxiliary Landing Field Oceana. On August 17, 1943, Oceana was commissioned an auxiliary air station with Lieutenant Jesse Arthur Fairley in command. Throughout the war, young men reported to Oceana to train for combat in the Pacific, where most were headed, or Europe and Africa. As Bellinger thus observed, his planes and pilots, trained at Norfolk, Oceana, Pungo or any number of other outlying Hampton Roads airfields, were in combat "from Dunkeswell to Dakar" and "from Reykjavik to Rio" and many far-flung places in between.

Operation Torch was the first major amphibious assault of World War II. On October 24, 1942, ninety-nine ships of Amphibious Force, Atlantic Fleet, also called Task Force 34, left Norfolk under the command of Rear Admiral Henry Kent Hewitt bound for the coast of North Africa. Admiral Royal Eason Ingersoll, commander in chief of the United States Atlantic Fleet, observed the task force's departure from Hampton Roads (shown here). *Courtesy of the Hampton Roads Naval Museum.*

Grumman TBF-1 Avengers fly formation over the Norfolk operating area in September 1942. Several Avenger squadrons were subsequently assigned to what was then Naval Auxiliary Air Station (NAAS) Oceana. The picture was taken by Horace Bristol, a member of Captain Edward Steichen's Naval Aviation Photographic Unit. *Courtesy of the National Archives and Records Administration.*

Above: A Martin PBM-3 Mariner is shown anchored in the water off Naval Air Station Norfolk in late summer 1942. The PBM-3 Mariner differed from earlier versions of the aircraft with its extended engine nacelles and strut-girded wing floats, which are outside the frame of this picture. This aircraft was powered by two 1,700-horsepower Wright R-2600-12 engines. *Courtesy of the Hampton Roads Naval Museum.*

Right: The USS *Ranger* (CV-4) was based in the Atlantic during World War II, where it played a decisive role in Operation Torch, the 1942 invasion of North Africa. But the carrier also ferried hundreds of United States Army fighter planes overseas. *Ranger* delivered the Lockheed P-38 Lightnings shown here to the Army Air Force in April 1944. *Official United States Navy Photograph.*

Black Seabees, members of naval construction battalions, trained at Norfolk Naval Base's Camp Allen and Little Creek's Camp Bradford during World War II. Camp Bradford was about half of the present Little Creek Naval Amphibious Base, established in 1945 and now designated Joint Expeditionary Training Base Little Creek–Fort Story. Little Creek consolidated four bases built during World War II: the Amphibious Training Base, the Naval Frontier Base and Camps Bradford and Shelton. But it also consisted of three annexes named for the former owners of the property: Shelton on the east, Bradford in the center and Whitehurst to the west. The men shown in this photograph, taken in 1942, practiced landing tactics at Camp Bradford, where they also trained in military drill. *Courtesy of the National Archives and Records Administration.*

Though the United States Navy had acquired the land, paved runways and had aviators flying out of Oceana before the outbreak of World War II, it was not officially established as an auxiliary air station until August 17, 1943, the day this picture was taken. The official ceremony drew the attendance of Rear Admiral Patrick Neison Lynch Bellinger (far right), Naval Aviator No. 8 and commander, Naval Air Force Atlantic. Lieutenant Jesse Arthur Fairley, the air station's first commanding officer, is standing center. *Official United States Navy Photograph.*

This September 17, 1943 picture of the aftermath of an explosion at Naval Air Station Norfolk shows hangar doors blown clear of buildings, fires raging and structures obliterated. Twenty-four aerial depth bombs accidentally rolled off an overloaded munitions trailer and exploded near hangars V-1 and V-2. Thirty navy personnel were killed, including one woman, Seaman Second Class (Sea2c) Elizabeth Korensky, who became the first WAVE to die in the line of duty during the war. *Courtesy of the author.*

Four hundred people were injured and office buildings were rocked in downtown Norfolk by the September 1943 blast. Glass shattered in buildings across the air station. Fifteen buildings—including the old public works office, six barracks, thirty-three aircraft, hangar V-30 and the Chief Petty Officers' Club—were destroyed. Hangars V-1 and V-2 were so heavily damaged that they had to be razed and rebuilt. This was the worst tragedy that ever struck the air station. *Courtesy of the author.*

A ground crewman secured the wing of this Bombing Squadron Eight (VB-8) Curtiss SB2C Helldiver in December 1943 at Naval Air Station Norfolk. *Official United States Navy Photograph.*

The enlisted barracks on Oceana's North Station were awash in mud when this photograph was taken in 1944. The aircraft on the flight line are Vought F4U-1D Corsairs and Grumman F6F Hellcats. *Official United States Navy Photograph.*

A canteen stocked with cigars and cigarettes, books and sodas was established on Oceana for the convenience of pilots and ground officers during World War II. While many of the items were for sale, others had been provided free of charge, including comic books and pinup girl magazines, for the base's officers. This picture was taken April 30, 1948. *Official United States Navy Photograph.*

A crew party was held in the summer of 1944 at Fleet Recreation Park, located just outside the perimeter of Naval Station Norfolk at Ninetieth Street and Hampton Boulevard. The park was established at the end of 1943 to accommodate the recreational needs of sailors, marines and their families. *Courtesy of the author.*

Although this picture of workers balancing aircraft propellers in Shop 6422, Building LP-21, was taken on May 7, 1947, the task had been part of day-to-day operations at Norfolk's Assembly and Repair since its inception as the Construction and Repair Department in 1918. *Official United States Navy Photograph.*

Medal of Honor recipient Commander David McCampbell was the United States Navy's leading ace of all time with his thirty-four World War II combat victories. He spent much of his career in Hampton Roads attached to aircraft carriers and squadrons preparing for war in the Pacific. He earned the Medal of Honor during his tour as commanding officer of Carrier Air Group Fifteen—the "Fabled Fifteen"—at the first and second battles of the Philippine Sea, the former also referred to as the Great Marianas Turkey Shoot. On that day, June 19, 1944, McCampbell shot down seven enemy aircraft, thus becoming "an ace in a day." But he bettered this achievement on October 24, 1944, when he shot down nine enemy aircraft in one flight, and that feat has never been repeated in combat aviation. McCampbell (in the cockpit) is pictured with his plane captain, Chet Owens, in November 1944. His Grumman F6F-5 Hellcat *Minsi III* displays all thirty-four of his combat kills. *Courtesy of the National Museum of Naval Aviation.*

A Grumman F4F Wildcat was returned from combat duty for maintenance at Naval Air Station Norfolk's Assembly and Repair Department. The sign on its fuselage tells the fighter's story. This Wildcat had destroyed a Japanese merchant vessel and a Vichy French ship before coming off the line. "The performance by this plane and its pilot, and others," it read, "depends on the work done here. Congratulations, F4F Wildcat, and may you soon again return to 'business as usual.'" Government censors removed mention of the specific aircraft model, although it was likely a -3 or -4 when this picture was taken in 1944. *Courtesy of the Hampton Roads Naval Museum.*

When it was launched at Newport News Shipbuilding on February 7, 1944, the *Ticonderoga* became one of twenty-four *Essex*-class aircraft carriers built during World War II for the United States Navy. USS *Ticonderoga* (CV-14) was commissioned at the Norfolk Navy Yard on May 8, 1944, with Captain Dixie Kiefer in command. The carrier saw intense combat in the last year of World War II in the Pacific. *Ticonderoga*'s enlisted men, shown here, celebrated on hearing news of Japan's unconditional surrender. This photograph was taken August 14, 1945. *Courtesy of the National Archives and Records Administration.*

Navy pilots headed down the Naval Air Station Norfolk flight line to their Goodyear FG-1D Corsairs about 1944. *Official United States Navy Photograph.*

A late arrival to Oceana, probably sometime during the spring or summer of 1945, was VT-97A, a torpedo bombing squadron equipped with the Grumman TBM-1C Avenger. Enlisted maintenance crew were photographed working on the squadron's Avengers on the Oceana flight line. *Courtesy of the author.*

The crew of the *Essex*-class aircraft carrier USS *Bennington* (CVA-20) spelled out the name of the sunken battleship USS *Arizona* (BB-39) as *Bennington* passed directly by its future memorial site on May 31, 1958. The *Arizona* memorial was then under construction and is today a lasting remembrance to those aboard it who lost their lives in the Japanese attack on Pearl Harbor, December 7, 1941. *Bennington* was commissioned on August 6, 1944, and decommissioned on November 8, 1946. But it was later modernized and recommissioned as an attack carrier on November 13, 1952, and served with the Norfolk-based Atlantic Fleet until reassignment to the Pacific. *Bennington* was redesignated an antisubmarine carrier (CVS) on June 30, 1959, and decommissioned for the last time on January 15, 1970. *Official United States Navy Photograph.*

Chapter 10

The Navy Capital of the World

The post–World War II era brought significant changes to the organization and mission of the navy in Hampton Roads. These changes were largely precipitated by a comprehensive review of the United States armed forces for the purpose of reorganization specified by an armed forces reorganization act approved by Congress and put into motion on December 1, 1947, when the unified United States Atlantic Command was established and its headquarters collocated to the United States Atlantic Fleet (COMLANTFLT) in Norfolk, Virginia. Admiral William Henry Purnell Blandy, commander in chief, United States Atlantic Fleet (CINCLANTFLT), thus became the first commander in chief, United States Atlantic Command (CINCLANT), a title that made Blandy and each of his successors dual-hatted, and later triple-hatted, until the 1985 Goldwater-Nichols Act separated the U.S. Atlantic Command from the U.S. Atlantic Fleet. But for decades after the North Atlantic Treaty Organization (NATO) made the decision to establish Allied Command, Atlantic under the command of an American four-star admiral with headquarters in Norfolk as of January 30, 1952, the work of three men belonged to just one. Norfolk was, after all, the home of the principal navy command tasked to defend the North Atlantic. A few months later, on April 10, 1952, Admiral Lynde Dupuy McCormick, commander in chief, United States Atlantic Command and United States Atlantic Fleet, added another title when he became the first supreme allied commander, Atlantic (SACLANT). Admiral Wesley L. McDonald was the last American admiral to command all three organizations at the same time. The U.S. Atlantic Fleet was not separated from the U.S. Atlantic Command

and SACLANT until McDonald relinquished command of the fleet to Admiral Carlisle Albert Herman Trost on October 4, 1985.

The impact of decisions made in Washington continued to reshape the navy's footprint in Hampton Roads. Chairman of the Joint Chiefs of Staff General Colin L. Powell, among others, knew that the key to meeting the challenges of the future was refining how American armed services worked together in joint operations. He felt that a single, unified command based in the United States should be responsible for training forces from all services for joint operations. This unified command would supply ready joint forces to other unified commanders in chief anywhere in the world. The United States Atlantic Command fulfilled General Powell's vision in 1993 when it became the first unified command to serve as United States–based force trainer, integrator and provider. Under the new Unified Command Plan, signed by President William Jefferson Clinton on September 24, 1993, Atlantic Command assumed combatant command of the United States Army's Forces Command (FORSCOM), the United States Air Force's Air Combat Command (ACC), the United States Marine Corps Forces Command Atlantic (MARFORLANT) and the navy's Atlantic Fleet (CINCLANTFLT). In October 1999, the U.S. Atlantic Command became the United States Joint Forces Command (USJFCOM), retaining its Norfolk-based headquarters.

The navy's top command in Norfolk would have more change to come. Just over two weeks after the September 11, 2001 terrorist attacks that struck New York and Washington and took down an airliner in a Pennsylvania field, the chief of naval operations designated the commander in chief, U.S. Atlantic Fleet, as concurrent commander, U.S. Fleet Forces Command (COMUSFLTFORCOM), a new command responsible for the overall coordination, establishment and implementation of integrated requirements and policies for manning, equipping and training Atlantic and Pacific Fleet units during the inter-deployment training cycle. The title "commander in chief" wouldn't last much longer. Secretary of Defense Donald Rumsfeld directed that the title of "commander in chief" was intended only in reference to the president of the United States. Thus, on October 24, 2002, in a message to naval commanders in chief, the chief of naval operations changed the title of all fleet and shore commanders in chief to "commander." Less than four years later, with the nation deeply embroiled in the war in Iraq and Afghanistan, part of a greater global war on terrorism, the chief of naval operations disestablished COMUSFLTFORCOM and COMLANTFLT. What emerged was a USFLTFORCOM with a commander ordered to carry out the missions performed by both disestablished commands and to serve as primary advocate for fleet personnel, training, requirements, maintenance and operational issues, reporting administratively to the chief of naval operations and operationally to the USJFCOM. Admiral John B. Nathman led the October 31, 2006 ceremony that marked the official transition of U.S. Atlantic Fleet to U.S. Fleet Forces Command.

The navy's top-down review of its shore facilities at the end of World War II led to major changes, too. Less than a year after the Japanese surrender in Tokyo Bay, in March 1946, the chief of naval operations directed the commandant of the Fifth Naval District, who also held the position of commander, U.S. Naval Station, to include Naval Station Norfolk and Naval Air Station Norfolk as separate component commands under the umbrella of commandant, Naval Base Norfolk. The title "commandant" would give way to "commander, Naval Base Norfolk." Today, the proper title is "commander, Navy Region Mid-Atlantic." Over the years, there has been much debate about the Norfolk naval base's proper title. The base was officially known as Naval Operating Base (NOB) Norfolk until December 31, 1952. The next day, January 1, 1953, and ever since, it has been Naval Station Norfolk. As part of the navy's post–cold war drawdown in the 1990s, it realigned its Norfolk shore facilities under the sea service's broader regionalization initiative. Thus, on February 5, 1999, Naval Air Station Norfolk was merged with the adjacent naval station as a single installation to be called Naval Station Norfolk. Chambers Field is still there. Despite the loss of its "naval air station" designation, this storied airfield continues to make history. But it and the naval station are just two parts of a much larger 4,631-acre naval base complex that makes Norfolk home to the largest naval base in the world and, based on its supported military population, the largest military station in the world.

The aircraft carrier USS *Midway* (CVB-41) arrived at Naval Station Norfolk from a six-month deployment to the Mediterranean Sea on March 11, 1948. *Courtesy of the Sargeant Memorial Room, Norfolk Public Library.*

President Harry S. Truman returned from a diplomatic visit to Rio de Janeiro, Brazil, arriving at Naval Station Norfolk aboard the battleship USS *Missouri* (BB-63) on September 19, 1947. He took the presidential yacht *Williamsburg* back to Washington, D.C. *Courtesy of the Sargeant Memorial Room, Norfolk Public Library.*

Midway-class aircraft carrier USS *Franklin D. Roosevelt* (CVB-42) made history on July 21, 1946, when a McDonnell XFD-1 Phantom jet, craned aboard the ship before its departure from Norfolk, was launched from the carrier's flight deck off the Virginia Capes. Lieutenant Commander James J. Davidson became the first pilot to fly a jet from the deck of an American aircraft carrier. The XFD-1 was redesignated the FH-1 Phantom, the first of which would be delivered to VF-17A in 1947. Charles Borjes took this picture of the carrier before it left Norfolk for deployment to the Mediterranean on September 13, 1948. *Courtesy of the Sargeant Memorial Room, Norfolk Public Library.*

Santa was ferried to the flight deck of the escort carrier USS *Mindoro* (CVE-120) via helicopter on December 23, 1951. *Mindoro*, pier side at Naval Station Norfolk, held a Christmas party below deck for ship's company children. Santa was portrayed by Boatswain's Mate C.L. Jones. The picture was taken by *Virginian-Pilot* photographer Jim Mays. *Courtesy of the Sargeant Memorial Room, Norfolk Public Library.*

Navy Captain James Henry Flatley sent a letter home to the families of Naval Air Station Norfolk sailors on October 29, 1953, to tell them that the strength and efficiency of the air station "at these critical times in world history" rested in large measure on the morale and spirit of the crew. "You and I share," he told them, "the responsibility for keeping that morale and spirit at the highest point." Illustrative of his point, airmen from Fighter Squadron Twenty-one, later redesignated Attack Squadron Forty-three and then Fighter Squadron Forty-three Challengers, held a Christmas party on December 21, 1957, for their families at Naval Air Station Oceana. *Official United States Navy Photograph.*

The second USS *Norfolk* (DL-1) was the first destroyer leader of the United States Navy. Originally projected as a hunter-killer cruiser (CLK-1), it was laid down September 1, 1949, at New York Shipbuilding Corporation, Camden, New Jersey. *Norfolk*, sponsored by Betty King Duckworth, was launched on December 29, 1951, and commissioned March 4, 1953, with Captain Clarence Matheson Bowley in command. The first major American warship built after the construction boom of World War II, *Norfolk* was authorized in 1947 as an antisubmarine hunter-killer ship that could operate under all weather conditions. *Norfolk* carried the latest radar, sonar and other electronic devices. As a large destroyer leader designed on a light cruiser hull, it could carry a greater variety of detection gear than a destroyer. *Norfolk* is shown here making its way out of the Elizabeth River. *Courtesy of the author.*

Norfolk was assigned to the United States Atlantic Fleet after its February 1954 shakedown cruise and between 1955 and 1957 served successively as flagship for Commander Destroyer Flotillas 2, 4 and 6. During 1956 and 1957, it acted as flagship for Commander Destroyer Force, Atlantic Fleet. In June 1957, *Norfolk* participated in the International Fleet Review as flagship for Admiral Jerauld Wright, commander in chief of the Atlantic Fleet and Supreme Allied Commander Atlantic. *Norfolk*'s navy service ended with its decommissioning on January 15, 1970, and it was stricken from the Naval Vessel Register on September 1, 1974. The City of Norfolk presented its namesake ship with this silver plate on the occasion of its commissioning in March 1953. *Courtesy of the author.*

The *Iowa*-class battleship USS *Wisconsin* (BB-64) was commissioned on April 16, 1944, at the Philadelphia Navy Yard. "Wisky" was the second American battleship to bear this name. BB-64's first commanding officer was Captain Earl Everett Stone, a Milwaukee native. The ship saw intense combat action in the Pacific during World War II. As the nation slipped into the euphoria of postwar peace, it was decommissioned and mothballed pier side at Newport News, Virginia, on July 1, 1948, after only four years and three months of active service to the fleet. Wisky's sleep was brief; it was restored to active duty during the Korean Conflict and remained in this status until March 8, 1958, when Wisky was again mothballed. *Wisconsin*'s absence left the navy without a battleship in the fleet for the first time since 1895. Wisky is shown here during an overhaul at Norfolk Naval Shipyard that began September 24, 1952. *Courtesy of Dominic Menta.*

USS *Wisconsin* (BB-64) fired a nine-gun salvo from its sixteen-inch guns on January 19, 1955, shown here, during Operation Springboard. Thirty years passed from the time *Wisconsin* was mothballed in March 1958 until it would see action again. Wisky waited. A handful of visionary naval strategists in the early 1980s concluded that the *Iowa*-class battleships were valuable capital ships. Wisky was dusted off, its propulsion and weapon systems updated and crew spaces refurbished. On October 22, 1988, it was recommissioned. Wisky left Naval Station Norfolk on August 7, 1990, for the Persian Gulf in support of Operation Desert Shield and, soon after, Operation Desert Storm. On September 30, 1991, it was decommissioned for the third and last time at Norfolk. While not the place of its birth, Norfolk has given the *Wisconsin* a new life. Wisky is now pier side in downtown Norfolk, a fitting and lasting memorial to the thousands of sailors who have served in the navy capital of the world. *Courtesy of Dominic Menta.*

President John F. Kennedy visited Naval Air Station Oceana on April 13, 1962, the first stop on his tour of United States Navy and Marine Corps installations in the Norfolk area. He was accompanied on the visit by Vice President Lyndon B. Johnson; Secretary of Defense Robert S. McNamara; Secretary of Commerce Luther B. Hodges; Chairman of the Joint Chiefs of Staff General Lyman L. Lemnitzer; and Commander of the Atlantic Fleet Admiral Robert L. Dennison, shown here conferring with the president. *Official United States Navy Photograph.*

Sailors prepare a drone antisubmarine helicopter (DASH) DSN-3 remote control helicopter aboard the USS *Lind* (DD-703), berthed at the Naval Station Norfolk destroyer-submarine piers on July 15, 1963. Drones started deploying aboard navy ships, largely destroyers, in 1963. A DASH training unit was established on April 1, 1971, at Fleet Antiair Warfare Training Center, Dam Neck Fleet Combat Training Center, Virginia Beach, Virginia. But just a few months later, on July 1, DASH aircraft were phased out of service. *Official United States Navy Photograph.*

This oblique view of the east portion of the Portsmouth Naval Hospital complex shows, in the middle ground, Medical Wards A, B and C, Portsmouth Naval Hospital Building and Hospital Point, and foreground, the gardener's toolshed, service building, garage and Medical Officers' Quarters C and B. The picture was taken looking north from the roof of the 1960 high-rise hospital building. *Courtesy of the Library of Congress Historic American Buildings Survey/Historical American Engineering Record.*

Captain Richard J. De Prez, Naval Air Station Norfolk commanding officer, stands in front of the *Apollo 7* command module on October 25, 1968. *Apollo 7*, the first manned flight test of third-generation American spacecraft, was deactivated at the air station's hangar LP-2 after its return from an eleven-day orbital flight manned by astronauts Command Pilot Walter Marty Schirra Jr., Command Module Pilot Donn Fulton Eisele and Lunar Module Pilot Ronnie Walter Cunningham. *Official United States Navy Photograph.*

Master Chief Aircrew Survival Equipmentman (PRCM) Forrest V. Miller donned a full-pressure suit, ready to test a new escape trainer at the Naval Air Station Norfolk Aviation Physiological Unit, circa 1965. *Official United States Navy Photograph.*

Air shows at Naval Air Station Norfolk, now Chambers Field, Naval Station Norfolk, drew tens of thousands of visitors to their static displays, military flight demonstrations and civilian aerobatic performers. This air show, photographed in the 1970s, clearly shows the huge draw of these events. *Official United States Navy Photograph.*

Vice President George Herbert Walker Bush led the inspection of a United States Marine Corps honor guard at Naval Station Norfolk Pier 12 in conjunction with ceremonies in his honor. The date was September 2, 1984, and Bush was nearing the end of his first term as President Ronald Reagan's vice president. He is followed by the honor guard officer and Secretary of the Navy John Lehman. *Official United States Navy Photograph.*

A Grumman E-2C Hawkeye piloted by Commander Joseph J. George, then executive officer of Carrier Airborne Early Warning Squadron 124 (VAW-124) Bear Aces, is catapulted off the deck of the aircraft carrier USS *Theodore Roosevelt* (CVN-71) on December 29, 1990. The *Roosevelt* departed Norfolk on December 28, headed to the Persian Gulf in support of Operation Desert Storm. *Courtesy of Carrier Airborne Early Warning Squadron One Hundred Twenty-Four.*

Commander in Chief of the United States Atlantic Fleet and Supreme Allied Commander Atlantic (SACLANT) Admiral Leon A. Edney (left) welcomed home Commander Robert E. Davis, commanding officer of Fighter Squadron Thirty-Two (VF-32) Swordsmen, to Naval Air Station Oceana on March 27, 1991. Carrier Air Wing Three (CVW-3) and Carrier Air Wing Seventeen (CVW-17) had just returned from the Persian Gulf in support of Operation Desert Storm. The Swordsmen were attached to CVW-3 aboard the USS *John F. Kennedy* (CV-67) and flew the Grumman F-14B Tomcat. *Official United States Navy Photograph.*

Three Oceana-based aviators (left to right), Lieutenants Robert Wetzel, Lawrence R. Slade and Jeffrey N. Zaun, were shot down and taken prisoners of war by the Iraqis during Operation Desert Storm. They were among ten allied prisoners of war, six of them American, repatriated to the International Committee of the Red Cross by Baghdad on March 4, 1991. Wetzel and Zaun were shot down in their Attack Squadron Thirty-Five (VA-35) Black Panthers A-6E Intruder on January 18, 1991. Slade was the backseater in a Fighter Squadron One Hundred Three (VF-103) Sluggers Tomcat F-14B when he and his pilot, Lieutenant Devon Jones, ejected on January 21. Jones was rescued. This picture was taken shortly after all had recovered and returned to Oceana for a formal ceremony held in their honor. *Official United States Navy Photograph.*

Vice President Al Gore addressed the crowd gathered at Newport News Shipbuilding for the christening of the aircraft carrier *John C. Stennis* (CVN-74) on November 11, 1993. *Courtesy of Naval Air Force Atlantic.*

Four Grumman A-6E Intruders from four Naval Air Station Oceana squadrons flew over the Wright Brothers Memorial at Kill Devil Hills, North Carolina, in August 1994. These aircraft—and their squadrons—represented the last of a breed. The Intruder was phased out completely in the years after this picture was taken. Shown here are jets from Attack Squadron Forty-Two (VA-42) Green Pawns, *top left*, which changed its squadron name to Thunderbolts prior to disestablishment on September 30, 1994; Attack Squadron Thirty-Five (VA-35) Black Panthers, *bottom left*, disestablished January 31, 1995; Attack Squadron Eighty-Five (VA-85) Black Falcons, *bottom right*, disestablished September 29, 1994; and Attack Squadron Seventy-Five (VA-75) Sunday Punchers, *top right*, disestablished February 28, 1997, which also marked the end of Intruder operations on the East Coast. *Official United States Navy Photograph.*

Oceana-based Fighter Squadron Eighty-Four (VF-84) Jolly Rogers F-14B Tomcats were photographed in January 1995 making a bombing run on the practice range at Vieques Island, Puerto Rico. *Official United States Navy Photograph.*

A Strike Fighter Squadron Eighty-Three (VFA-83) Rampagers F/A-18 Hornet, assigned to Carrier Air Wing Seventeen (CVW-17) aboard USS *Dwight D. Eisenhower* (CVN-68), was taken in September 1997. Naval Air Station Oceana became the home of Strike Fighter Weapons School and Strike Fighter Squadron One Hundred Six (VFA-106), the F/A-18 Hornet and F/A-18 Super Hornet fleet replacement squadron (FRS), Strike Fighter Wing Atlantic and six Hornet squadrons on July 1, 1999. *Courtesy of Strike Fighter Wing Atlantic.*

This stacked formation of F/A-18 Hornets, each one from a different Atlantic Fleet strike fighter squadron, consists of (from front left, foreground) VFA-37 Bulls, VFA-34 Blue Blasters, VFA-81 Sunliners, VFA-131 Wildcats, VFA-136 Knighthawks, VFA-105 Gunslingers, VFA-83 Rampagers and VFA-106 Gladiators. The picture was taken in September 1997 for Boeing. Most of the aircraft are sporting their CAG bird colors. *Courtesy of Strike Fighter Wing Atlantic.*

The United States Atlantic Fleet Band, established in 1945 to support the headquarters of the fleet's commander in chief, remains the primary musical representation of today's United States Fleet Forces Command and is the largest of the navy's twelve fleet bands. The band was photographed during its April 24, 2002 performance at the traditional flag-raising ceremony that was held annually at the headquarters of Supreme Allied Commander Atlantic (SACLANT)/North Atlantic Treaty Organization (NATO) to honor the Norfolk International Azalea Festival's most honored nation and its queen. The azalea festival was renamed the Norfolk NATO Festival in 2009, and the practice of selecting a queen has been discontinued. *Official SACLANT/NATO Photograph.*

Sources

Every effort was made to consult primary source material in the compilation of this volume, most especially official government and United States Navy archives, and including publications, records, original accounts, scrapbooks and photographic files found in the National Archives and Records Administration (NARA), Library of Congress (LOC), Department of Defense, Department of the Navy, Naval Historical Center, National Museum of Naval Aviation, Hampton Roads Naval Museum, Portsmouth Naval Shipyard Museum, Sargeant Memorial Room, Norfolk Public Library and innumerable command histories, including unit and squadron histories and photographs. The rest was derived from the author's prior writings pertaining to and knowledge of the United States Navy and Marine Corps and her own collection of original documents and photographs. The author acknowledges the wealth of information gleaned from individual interviews.